The Intrareligious Dialogue

Revised Edition

RAIMON PANIKKAR

Paulist Press
New York, N.Y. • Mahwah, N.J.

Cover design by Cindy Dunne

Library of Congress Cataloging-in-Publication Data

Panikkar, Raimon, 1918–
    The intrareligious dialogue / Raimon Panikkar. — Rev. ed.
        p.   cm.
    Includes bibliographical references and index.
    ISBN 0–8091–3763–1 (alk. paper)
    1. Religions—Relations.   2. Christianity and other religions.
    I. Title.
    BL410.P36   1999
    291.1'72—dc21   98-49313
                                                                        CIP

Published by Paulist Press
997 Macarthur Boulevard
Mahwah, New Jersey 07430

www.paulistpress.com

Printed and bound in the United States of America

Contents

List of Abbreviations

AV	*Atharva Veda*
BG	*Bhagavad Gītā*
BS	*Brahma Sūtra*
BU	*Bṛhadāraṇyaka Upaniṣad*
CU	*Chāndogya Upaniṣad*
JabU	*Jābāla Upaniṣad*
MB	*Mahābhārata*
MaitU	*Maitrī Upaniṣad*
P.G.	Migne, J. P. *Patrologia Cursus Completus, Series Graeca* (Paris: Migne, 1857–66)
P.L.	Migne, J. P. *Patrologia Cursus Completus, Series Latina* (Paris: Migne, 1844–55)
RV	*Ṛg Veda*
SB	*Śatapatha Brāhmaṇa*
SU	*Śvetāśavatara Upaniṣad*
TB	*Taittirīya Brāhmaṇa*

For the Bible the usual abbreviations are employed.

The Intrareligious Dialogue

A CCIDIT UT POST DIES ALIQUOT, FORTE EX DIUTURNA continuata meditatione, visio quaedam eidem zeloso manifestaretur, ex qua elicuit quod paucorum sapientium omnium talium diversitatum quae in religionibus per orbem observantur peritia pollentium unam posse facilem quandam concordantiam reperiri, ac per eam in religione perpetuam pacem convenienti ac veraci medio constitui.

—Nicolai de Cusa
De Pace seu Concordantia Fidei I, 1*

It happened after some days, perhaps as the fruit of an intense and sustained meditation, that a vision appeared to this ardently devoted Man. In this vision it was manifested that by means of a few sages versed in the variety of religions that exist throughout the world it could be possible to reach a certain peaceful concord. And it is through this concord that a lasting peace in religion may be attained and established by convenient and truthful means.

*Cf. R. Llull, *Liber de quinque sapientibus* expressing the same idea almost two centuries before.

Preface to the New Edition

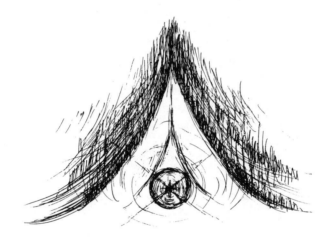

THE FIRST EDITION OF THIS BOOK HAS HAD A SECOND REVISED indian reprint and spanish, german, and french translations.

The second english edition has been revised with the addition of four more chapters and amounts to another book and a third english edition.

The *motto* "The Sermon on the Mount of Intrareligious Dialogue," preceding the chapters, expresses the basic human attitude required for a fruitful dialogue.

The author wishes to thank the Paulist Press, which has overcome the idolatry of our accelerated times, which worships news and novelty. The issues of this book not only represent a lifelong occupation of its author; they also claim to be an inescapable concern of the reader: one's personal fulfillment.

R.P.
Tavertet (Catalunya)
Easter 1998.

A Note to the Reader

THE AUTHOR OF THIS BOOK CAN BOAST OF CENTURIES OF MATRI-archal pedigree still alive in Kerala. This is another reason for not allowing males to usurp the monopoly on *Adam, puruṣa, anthrôpos, homo, Mensch* . . . and split the human race into the dialectical dichotomy of divisive language: male/fe-male, man/wo-man, ish/isha. . . . Furthermore, to substitute "person" for Man will not do for most of the nonwestern cultures, which react negatively to this loaded and artificial word, nor will the expression "human being" convince those cultures that do not have the genius of the western mind (some may call it an obsession) for classifying everything. For many, the expression "human being" denies the uniqueness of every one of us; it is as if to say, among the many beings that exist in this world, humans are just a species, and among them the individual just a unit in the series. This attitude is felt to be contrary to human dignity, for we are not replaceable beings; each one of us is not a means for something else, but an end in himself—and thus nonclassifiable. For this and many other reasons the author avoids divisive language and states that the word Man stands for that unique Being incarnated in any one of us between Heaven and Earth, as the immense majority of human traditions understand the mystery of Man.

Preface

οὐκ ἐμοῦ,
ἀλλὰ τοῦ λόγου ἀκούσαντας

not to me,
but listening to the *logos* . . .
—Herakleitos Fragm. 50

D IALOGUE AS A HUMAN AND HUMANE ACT HAS NEVER BEEN so indispensable in all fields of life as in our age of endemic individualism. All our glib talk of "global village" takes place on artificial screens under lock and key, and the copyrights of "privileged" individuals jealous of their privacy moving around at high speed in bunkers called cars that cause over one million casualties per year. Either we discover again and anew the neighbor in flesh and blood or we are heading toward a disaster of cosmic proportions, as the word itself indicates *(dis-astrum)*. Our individual self-sufficiency is in crisis. We constantly run up one against the other, but we hardly have time to find our neighbor—because we do not find ourselves, being too busy with "businesses" of all sorts. *"Qui enim se cognoscit, in se omnia cognoscet"* (Who knows one-self, knows all things in one-self)—said the ancients, as formulated by Pico della Mirandola in his *Oratio.*

Our dealings with others are mostly either on the merely objective or on the purely subjective level, that is, either rational encounters or sentimental meetings. In the first case, we engage in *'dialectical dialogues'*. We meet on supposedly neutral ground: the *'arena'* of doctrines and opinions. In the second case, we engage in *'erotic dialogues'*. We meet on terrains of sympathy and antipathy at different levels: the *agora* of "personal" relationships.

Both encounters are part and parcel of our human condition, but if kept asunder, they are insufficient for a full human realization. Man is more than a thinking machine and a bundle of desires. The world is more than an objective fact, and the others more than separated individuals. "*Semper occulta quaedam est concatenatio*" (There is always a certain hidden connection between all things), to cite another phrase of Pico's in a wider context (*Opera omnia*, ed. Basileae, 1572, p. 235), which expresses what other traditions have termed as universal *harmonia, perichôrêsis, pratītiya-samutpāda, sarvam-sarvātmakam,* and the like. Our relationship with the other is not an external link but belongs to our innermost constitution, be it with the earth, the living beings—especially the humans—or the divine. The entire reality presents a '*theoanthropocosmic*' or, better sounding, a '*cosmotheandric*' nature.

When we limit our field to human relationships, we see that the other is not just a producer of ideas with which we agree more or less, or just a bearer of affinities that make possible a number of transactions; it is neither a mere (other) subject nor a mere (other) object. It is a person who is not my ego, and yet it belongs to my Self. This is what makes communication and communion possible. This awareness is the dawn of the '*dialogical dialogue*'. The thou emerges as different from the non-I.

When this encounter touches the depths of our intimate beliefs, when it reaches the ultimate questions of the meaning of life, in whatever sense, we have the '*religious dialogical dialogue*'. Oftentimes this dialogue does not go beyond doctrinal levels or emotional projections. This is the '*interreligious dialogue*', which is generally carried on by experts or representatives of different belief-systems or artistic sensitivities.

When the dialogue catches hold of our entire person and removes our many masks, because something stirs within us, we begin the '*intrareligious dialogue*'. This is the internal dialogue triggered by the thou who is not in-different to the I. Something stirs in the inmost recesses of our being that we do not often dare to verbalize too loudly. That movement can lead to a purifying individual solitude or to a destructive individualistic isolation. The walls of "microdoxies" tumble down, and we can be buried under the rubble unless we succeed in clearing away the stones to build our house anew. The temptation may be twofold. For the powerful, it is to build a tower of Babel for the sake of unity—be it called one God, religion, or culture, or one world government, democracy, or market. The human scale is lost. For the powerless the temptation is to construct for oneself an isolated shell instead of a home open to community. Again, the human scale is lost.

In brief, the intrareligious dialogue is itself a religious act—an act that neither unifies nor stifles but re-links us (in all directions). It takes place in the core of our being in our quest for salvific truth—in whatever sense we may understand these too-loaded words. We engage in such a dialogue not only looking above, toward a transcendent reality, or behind, toward an original tradition, but also horizontally, toward the world of other people who may believe they have found other paths leading to the realization of human destiny. The search becomes an authentic prayer, a prayer open in all directions.

The first steps of the intrareligious dialogue hardly make any sound. They take place in the depths of the person. This dialogue is *open.* It is no longer locked in the jail of egotism; it is open to the religiousness of our neighbors. How else could we love them as ourselves? Their beliefs become a personal religious question. It is also *profound.* It is no longer concerned with mere formulations (of our own tradition or of other people). It is a personal question concerning the meaning of reality—salvific truth, as we said before.

The intrareligious dialogue is an internal dialogue in which one struggles with the angel, the *daimôn,* and oneself. How can we have access to the whole of a liberating truth if our neighbors seem to have other beliefs, which are sometimes totally incompatible with our own convictions?

This internal dialogue is neither a monologue nor a simple soliloquy with "God;" nor a meditation on the partner's belief or on another religion. It is not research into a different worldview out of curiosity, or with a sympathetic mind. In this dialogue, we are in search of salvation, and we accept being taught by others, not only by our own clan. We thus transcend the more or less unconscious attitude of private property in the religious realm. Intrareligious dialogue is, of its very nature, an act of assimilation—which I would call eucharistic. It tries to assimilate the transcendent into our immanence.

But, one might say, the source of truth is found in God, or at least in transcendence, and not in Man. Truth manifests itself in enlightenment, the salvific experience, transcendence, or even evidence. At any event, this truth is not the result of my whim; it has a certain supraindividual character, be its name God, Love, Humanity, or Ignorance. Why then seek religious truth among human opinions? Isn't there the beginning of a religious apostasy in intrareligious dialogue? Shouldn't I first try to understand better the riches of my tradition before venturing into unknown ways, trying to understand what others have said and thought? Can I be an orthodox vedantin or a roman catholic if I lend an attentive ear to

foreign sirens? Do I no longer believe in the fullness of Revelation crystallized in my tradition? Do I even have a right to serve myself a religious
cocktail according to my own taste? In a word, doesn't intrareligious dialogue smack of a tendency toward eclecticism that betrays my lack of
faithfulness and my shallowness?

It is precisely because these important queries have been ignored or
interpreted as sectarian and fanatical attitudes that there is a growing pro-
liferation of so-called new religious movements of all types. One is
attracted by what is exotic; one misunderstands the meaning of newness
and becomes uprooted. This explains both the attraction of the East for
western people and the exodus of young orientals to the centers of science
and technology. One should never mention the impact of the East on the
West without, at the same time, underlining the greater impact of the West
on the East—which westerners sometimes seem to take for granted.

Undoubtedly, it is imperative to know first of all one's own tradition.
However, to affirm contentedly that we should be able to find in our own
tradition all that we are seeking is neither convincing nor sufficient. In the
first place, very often we only discover the profound meaning of our own
world after we have tasted something exotically different. One discovers
"home, sweet home" when one returns from elsewhere. The prophet is
almost always someone who has come from the outside, and often from
exile. In the second place, to think of ourselves, even collectively, as self-
sufficient implies a certain condemnation of others. We respect them and
even accept that they may have their own subjective justification, but we
consider them to be in error in whatever does not conform to our own criteria of truth, which are set up as absolute parameters. Even those who
believe in an absolute Revelation must admit that their interpretation of
that Revelation is limited and hence incomplete.

All this is very complex, but intrareligious dialogue transcends the
purely sociological and historical levels. It belongs also to the realm of
philosophical anthropology, if we wish to force it into categories. It is, in a
word, a constitutive element of Man, who is a knot in a net of relationships, that is, a person—and not an isolated individual, conscious atom,
or mere number—within an undifferentiated democratic complex. It is
our human nature that beckons to discover within ourselves the whole
human world and also the entire reality. We are constitutively open—not
only because the whole universe can penetrate us, but also because we can
permeate all of reality. *Anima quodammodo omnia* (the human soul is, in a
certain way, all things) said the scholastics, repeating Aristotle. When we
speak of Man as a microcosm, this does not mean that we are another

world in miniature, side-by-side with a multiplicity of small worlds; it means that Man is the "miniaturization" of the (only) world, that we are the world on our human scale. The other is certainly an *alius*, another nucleus in the network of relationships, an "other" individual, but not an *aliud*, another "thing," another (human) atom with no relatedness other than that defined by space or time narrowly considered as external elements to the human monads.

Intrareligious dialogue, by helping us discover the "other" in ourselves—is it not written, love your neighbor as yourself, as your "same" self?—contributes to the personal realization and mutual fecundation of the human traditions that can no longer afford to live in a state of isolation, separated from each other by walls of mutual mistrust, or in a state of war that may be more or less camouflaged by emulation and competition. Even peaceful coexistence is often but one form of political strategy for maintaining the status quo—preferable, undoubtedly, to war.

All in all, the intrareligious dialogue is not a minor affair; it is neither a strategy for peace nor even a method for better understanding. It is all this, and more, because it implies, first of all, a vision of reality that is neither monistic nor dualistic or atomistic. I am not the other, nor is the other I, but we are together because we are all sharers of the word, as the Ṛg Veda (I, 164, 37) says. We *are* in dialogue.

"When two will be made one, both the inside and the outside, the outside and the inside, the superior and the inferior . . . then you will enter [into 'the Kingdom']," ways the Gospel of Thomas, 22. When I shall have discovered the atheist, the hindu and the christian in me, when I shall consider me and my sister as belonging to the same Self (Being, destiny, reality, mystery . . .), when the "other" will not feel alienated in me, nor I in the other . . . then we shall be closer to the Reign, *nirvāṇa*, realization, fullness, *śūnyāta*, . . .

Santa Barbara (California)
Pentecost 1983

Preface to the Original Edition

There is a long way, painful, but at the same time purifying, that is leading contemporary christian consciousness from a self-understanding of being a historically privileged people, bearing an exclusive or inclusive message of salvation for the entire world, to an awareness of self-identity that without weakening the strength of a conviction of uniqueness and fidelity to its own calling does make room for different ultimate and salvific human experiences.

For thirty years the author has written extensively on such problems. The present essays (most of them written in the "ghāts" of the Ganges) are here gathered as stepping stones of that way. They were written in the middle of the internal struggle of the ecclesial self-reflection. They have been detached from another collection of studies, *Myth, Faith and Hermeneutics* because although they complement the chapters of the other book, their internal unity appears clearer as an independent volume.

The Sermon on the Mount
of Intrareligious Dialogue

WHEN YOU ENTER INTO AN INTRARELIGIOUS DIALOGUE, DO NOT *think* beforehand what you have to believe.

When you *witness* to your faith, do not defend yourself or your vested interests, sacred as they may appear to you. Do like the birds in the skies: they sing and fly and do not defend their music or their beauty.

When you dialogue with somebody, look at your partner as a revelatory experience, as you would—and should—look at the lilies in the fields.

When you engage in intrareligious dialogue, try first to remove the beam in your own eye before removing the speck in the eye of your neighbor.

Blessed are you when you do not feel self-sufficient while being in dialogue.

Blessed are you when you trust the other because you trust in Me.

Blessed are you when you face misunderstandings from your own community or others for the sake of your fidelity to Truth.

Blessed are you when you do not give up your convictions, and yet you do not set them up as absolute norms.

Woe unto you, you theologians and academicians, when you dismiss what others say because you find it embarrassing or not sufficiently learned.

Woe unto you, you practitioners of religions, when you do not listen to the cries of the little ones.

Woe unto you, you religious authorities, because you prevent change and (re)conversion.

Woe unto you, religious people, because you monopolize religion and stifle the Spirit, which blows where and how she wills.

1

The Rhetoric of the Dialogue

... e aquí preseren comiat los tres savis la un de l'altre molt amablement e molt agradable; e cascú qués perdó a l'altre si havia dita contra sa lig nulla vilana paraula; e la un perdonà l'altre. E quan foren en ço que's volgren departir, la un savi dix:

—De la ventura que'ns és avenguda en la forest on venim, seguir-se-n'ha a nosaltres alcun profit. ¿Parria-us bo que, per la manera dels cinc arbres e per les deu condicions significades per lurs flors, cascun jorn una vegada, nos deputàssem,* e que seguíssem la manera que la dona d'Intel.ligència nos ha donada: e que tant de temps duràs nostra desputació tro que tots tres haguéssem una fe e una lig tan solament, e que enfre nós haguéssem manera d'honrar e servir la un L'altre, per ço

que enans nos puscam concordar? Car guerra treball e malvolença, e
donar dan e honta, empatxa los hòmens a ésser concordants en una
creença.

Ramon Llull

Libre del gentil e los tres savis (in finem)

(*)Sic, sed legendum 'desputàssem'.

. . . and here the three sages took leave of each other with great love and
in a very agreeable way: each of them asked forgiveness of the others in
case he might have proffered any unkind word against the religion of
the other; and each of them did pardon the others. And when they were
about to leave one of the sages said: Some profit should result from the
venture that has happened to us in the forest. Would it not be good that,
following the model of the five trees and the ten conditions represented
by their flowers, we could discuss once every coming day the indica-
tions given to us by Dame Intelligence? Our discussions should continue as long as necessary until we arrive at one faith and one religion
so that we will have a form of honoring each other and serving each
other. This would be the quickest way to come to our mutual concord.
For war, strained works, and ill will produce harm and shame, hinder-
ing people in their efforts to reach an agreement on one belief.

Ramon Llull, *Obres essencials,*
Barcelona (Editorial Selecta), vol. I, 1957, p. 1138.

THE CHAPTERS THAT FOLLOW DO NOT ELABORATE A THEORY
of the religious encounter. They are part of that very encounter. And
it is out of this praxis that I would like to propose the following *attitudes*
and *models* for the proper rhetoric in the meeting of religious traditions.

I do not elaborate now on the value of these attitudes or the merits of
these models. This would require studying the function and nature of the
metaphor as well as developing a theory of the religious encounter. I only
describe some attitudes and models, although I will probably betray my
sympathies in the form of critical considerations. The dialogue needs an
adequate rhetoric—in the classical sense of the word.

1. FIVE ATTITUDES

a. Exclusivism

A believing member of a religion in one way or another considers his own religion to be true. Now, the claim to truth has a certain built-in claim to exclusivity. If a given statement is true, its contradictory cannot also be true. And if a certain human tradition claims to offer a universal context for truth, anything contrary to that 'universal truth' will have to be declared false.

If, for instance, islām embodies the true religion, a 'non-islamic truth' cannot exist in the field of religion. Any long-standing religious tradition, of course, will have developed the necessary distinctions so as not to appear too blunt. It will say, for instance, that there are degrees of truth and that any 'religious truth', if it is really true, 'is' already a muslim one, although the people concerned may not be conscious of it. It will further distinguish an objective order of truth from a subjective one so that a person can be 'in good faith' and yet be in objective error, which as such will not be imputed against that person, and so forth.

This attitude has a certain element of heroism in it. You consecrate your life and dedicate your entire existence to something that is really worthy of being called a human cause, to something that claims to be not just a partial and imperfect truth, but a universal and even absolute truth. To be sure, an absolute God or Value has to be the final guarantee for such an attitude so that you do not follow it because of personal whims or because you have uncritically raised your point of view to an absolute value. It is God's rights you defend when asserting your religion as 'absolute religion.' This does not imply an outright condemnation of the beliefs of all other human beings who have not received the 'grace' of your calling. You may consider this call a burden and a duty (to carry vicariously the responsibility for the whole world) more than a privilege and a gift. Who are we to put conditions on the Almighty?

On the other hand, this attitude presents its difficulties. First, it carries with it the obvious danger of intolerance, hybris, and contempt for others. "We belong to the club of truth." It further bears the intrinsic weakness of assuming an almost purely logical conception of truth and the uncritical attitude of an epistemological naiveté. Truth is many-faceted, and even if you assume that God speaks an exclusive language, everything depends on your understanding of it so that you may never really know whether your interpretation is the *only* right one. To recur to a superhuman instance in the discussion between two religious beliefs does not solve any question, for it is often the case that God 'speaks' also to others, and both partners relying on God's authority will always need the human mediation so that ultimately God's authority depends on Man's interpretation (of the divine revelation).

As a matter of fact, although there are many de facto remnants of an exclusivistic attitude today, it is hardly defended de jure. To use the christian *skandalon,* for instance, to defend christianity would amount to the very betrayal of that saying about the "stumbling block." It would be the height of hypocrisy to condemn others and justify oneself using the scandal of God's revelation as a rationale for defending one's own attitude: divine revelation ceases to be a scandal for you (for you seem to accept it without scandal)—and you hurl it at others.

b. Inclusivism

In the present world context one can hardly fail to discover positive and true values—even of the highest order—outside of one's own tradition. Traditional religions have to face this challenge. "Splendid isolation" is no longer possible. The most plausible condition for the claim to truth of one's own tradition is to affirm at the same time that it includes at different levels all that there is of truth wherever it exists. The inclusivistic attitude will tend to reinterpret things in such a way as to make them not only palatable but also assimilable. Whenever facing a plain contradiction, for instance, it will make the necessary distinctions between different planes so as to be able to overcome that contradiction. It will tend to become a universalism of an existential or formal nature rather than of essential content. A doctrinal truth can hardly claim universality if it insists too much on specific contents because the grasping of the contents always implies a particular *'forma mentis'*. An attitude of tolerant admission of different planes will, on the contrary, have it easier. An umbrella pattern or a formal structure can easily embrace different thought-systems.

If vedānta, for example, is really the end and acme of all the Vedas, these latter understood as an expression of all types of ultimate revelation, it can seemingly affirm that all sincere human affirmations have a place in its scheme because they represent different stages in the development of human consciousness and have a value in the particular context in which they are said. Nothing is rejected and all is fitted into its proper place.

This attitude has a certain quality of magnanimity and grandeur in it. You can follow your own path and do not need to condemn the other. You can even enter into communion with all other ways of life, and if you happen to have the real experience of inclusivity, you may be at peace not only with yourself, but with all other human and divine ways as well. You can be concrete in your allegiances and universal in your outlook.

On the other hand, this attitude also entails some difficulties. First, it also presents the danger of hybris because it is only you who have the privilege of an all-embracing vision and tolerant attitude, you who allot to the others the place they must take in the universe. You are tolerant in your own eyes but not in the eyes of those who challenge your right to be on top. Furthermore, it has the intrinsic difficulties of an almost alogical conception of truth and a built-in inner contradiction when the attitude is spelled out in theory and praxis.

If this attitude allows for a variegated expression of 'religious truth' so as to be able to include the most disparate systems of thought, it is bound to make truth purely relative. Truth here cannot have an independent intellectual content, for it is one thing for the parsi and another for the vaiṣṇava, one thing for the atheist and another for the theist. So, it is also another thing for you—unless you jump outside the model because it is you who have the clue, you who find a place for all the different world views. But then your belief, conception, ideology, intuition, or whatever name we may call it becomes a supersystem the moment that you formulate it: you seem to understand the lower viewpoints and put them in their right places. You cannot avoid claiming for yourself a superior knowledge even if you deny that your conviction is another viewpoint. If you "say," furthermore, that your position is only the ineffable fruit of a mystical insight, the moment that you put it into practice nothing prevents another from discovering and formulating the implicit assumptions of that attitude. Ultimately you claim to have a fuller truth in comparison with all the others, who have only partial and relative truths.

As a matter of fact, although there are still many tendencies in several religious traditions that consider themselves all-inclusive, there are today only very few theoretical and philosophical formulations of a purely inclusivistic attitude. The claim of pluralism today is too strong to be so easily bypassed.

c. Parallelism

If your religion appears far from being perfect and yet it represents for you a symbol of the right path and a similar conviction seems to be the case for others, if you can neither dismiss the religious claim of the other nor assimilate it completely into your tradition, a plausible alternative is to assume that all are different creeds, which, in spite of meanderings and crossings, actually run parallel, to meet only in the ultimate, in the eschaton, at the very end of the human pilgrimage. Religions would then be parallel paths and our most urgent duty would be not to interfere with others, not to convert them or even to borrow from them, but to deepen our own respective traditions so that we may meet at the end and in the depths of our own traditions. Be a better christian, a better marxist, a better hindu and you will find unexpected riches and also points of contact with other people's ways.

This attitude presents very positive advantages. It is tolerant; it respects the others and does not judge them. It avoids muddy syncretisms and eclecticisms that concoct a religion according to our private tastes; it keeps the boundaries clear and spurs constant reform of one's own ways.

On the other hand, it too is not free of difficulties. First of all, it seems to go against the historical experience that the different religious and human traditions of the world have usually emerged from mutual interferences, influences, and fertilizations. It too hastily assumes, furthermore, that every human tradition has in itself all the elements for further growth and development; in a word, it assumes the self-sufficiency of every tradition and seems to deny the need or convenience of mutual learning or the need to walk outside the walls of one particular human tradition—as if in every one of them the entire human experience were crystallized or condensed. It flatters every one of us to hear that we possess *in nuce* all we need for a full human and religious maturity, but it splits the human family into watertight compartments, making any kind of conversion a real betrayal of one's own being. It allows growth but not mutation. Even if we run parallel to each other, are there not *sangama, prayāga,* affluents, inundations, natural and artificial dams, and above all, does not one and the same water flow 'heavenward' in the veins of the human being? Mere parallelism eschews the real issues.

Notwithstanding, this attitude presents on the other hand more prospects for an initial working hypothesis today. It carries a note of hope and patience at the same time; hope that we will meet at the end and patience that meanwhile we have to bear our differences. Yet when facing concrete problems of interferences, mutual influences, and even dialogue one cannot just wait until this *kalpa* comes to an end or the eschaton appears. All crossings are dangerous, but there is no new life without *maithuna.*

d. Interpenetration

The more we come to know the religions of the world, the more we are sensitive to the religiousness of our neighbor, all the more do we begin to surmise that in every one of us the other is somehow implied, and vice versa, that the other is not so independent from us and is somehow touched by our own beliefs. We begin to realize that our neighbor's religion not only challenges and may even enrich our own, but that ultimately the very differences that separate us are somewhat potentially within the world of my own religious convictions. We begin to accept that the other religion may complement mine, and we may even entertain the idea that in some particular cases it may well supplement some of my beliefs, provided that my religiousness remains an undivided whole. More and more we have the case of marxists accepting christian ideas, christians subscribing to hindu tenets, muslims absorbing buddhist views, and so on, and all the while remaining marxists, christians, and muslims. But there is still more than this: It looks as if we are today all intertwined and that without these particular religious links my own religion would be incomprehensible for me and even impossible. Religions are ununderstandable without a certain background of "religion." Our own religiousness is seen within the framework of our neighbor's. Religions do not exist in isolation but over against each other. There would be no hindu consciousness were it not for the fact of having to distinguish it from muslim and christian consciousness, for example. In a word, the relation between religions is neither of the type of exclusivism (only mine), or inclusivism (the mine embraces all the others), or parallelism (we are running independently toward the same goal), but one of a *sui generis perichôrêsis* or *circumincessio*, that is, of mutual interpenetration without the loss of the proper peculiarities of each religiousness.

The obvious positive aspect of this attitude is the tolerance, broadmindedness and mutual confidence that it inspires. No religion is totally foreign to my own; within our own religion we may encounter the religion of the other; we all need one another; in some way we are saying not just the same but mutually complementing and correcting things. And even when religions struggle for supplementation, they do it within a mutually acknowledged religious frame.

On the other hand, this attitude is also not free from dangers. First of all, one has to ask if this thinking is not a little wishful. Are we so sure of this interpenetration? So 'karma' and 'Providence' interpenetrate or exclude each other? On what grounds can we establish it? Is this attitude not already a modification of the self-understanding of the traditions themselves? This could be answered by justifying the role of creative hermeneutics. Each interpretation is a new creation. But can we say that such hermeneutics really exist in all the minutiae of the world religions? Or is it not a kind of new religiousness that makes selective use of the main tenets of the traditions while neglecting the others? There may be a religious universe, but is it sufficiently broad as to allow for insuperable incompatibilities?

But again this attitude may offer perspectives that the others lack. It may put us on a way that is open to all and that nobody should feel reluctant to enter. It can contribute to the spiritual growth of the partners: Even interpreting other beliefs as exaggeration or distortions of our own, we touch a more fundamental frame of reference, and without losing our identity, we weaken our assertive ego. It can contribute to a mutual enrichment within a synthesis. The values of the other tradition are not merely juxtaposed to those of our tradition but truly assimilated and integrated to our beliefs and in our own being. It is an open process.

e. Pluralism

We should stress here that we use this polysemic word not as a supersystem, which gives a more complete answer to the vexed problem of the relationship among religions, criticizing all the others as onesided, but as denoting an attitude. It is the attitude of not breaking the dialogue with the other opinions, because having renounced any absolutization, it keeps the intrareligious dialogue permanently open.

The aim of the intrareligious dialogue is understanding. It is not to win over the other or to come to a total agreement or a universal religion. The ideal is communication in order to bridge the gulfs of mutual ignorance and misunderstandings between the different cultures of the world, letting them speak and speak out their own insights in their own languages. Some may wish even to reach communion, but this does not imply at all that the aim is a uniform unity or a reduction of all the pluralistic variety of Man into one single religion, system, ideology, or tradition. Pluralism stands between unrelated plurality and a monolithic unity. It implies that the human condition in its present reality should not be neglected, let alone despised in favor of an ideal (?) situation of human uniformity. On the contrary, it takes our factual situation as real and affirms that in the actual polarities of our human existence we find our real being.

Pluralism takes very seriously the fact that during the last six to eight thousand years of human history our fellow beings have not come to an agreement concerning religious beliefs. Our ancestors were not unintelligent, nor were they blind partisans of the respective establishments. A certain evolutionistic thinking, making us believe that we are at the top of the spiritual insights of the human race and all the others were "undeveloped" smacks of modern hybris and ignorant naïvete.

For this very confidence it has in Man and not because of tired skepticism, the pluralistic attitude is not stuck at resolving the objective quandaries of religious divergencies and turns to the subjective, that is, human side of the problem. Could it not be that the dream of the mind to understand everything, because ultimately everything is intelligible, is a gratuitous and uncritical assumption? Pluralism is inclined to overcome the monopoly of the mental over everything. We are more, not less, than "rational." And perhaps the more realistic basis on which to ground human conviviality is not rational knowledge but loving awareness.

In other words, the pluralistic attitude dares not to accept the parmenidean dogma of the biunivocal correlation between thinking and being. We are aware of the unthinkable, for instance. Patience, tolerance, love, and the role of the heart are not accidental to human life and reveal to us aspects of ourselves and of reality that cannot be reduced *ad unum*— without for that matter having to accept duality.

Having dealt with this problem elsewhere, this brief description may suffice here.

* * * * *

I have described these five attitudes as examples of basic postures that when put to work become, of course, much more sophisticated. When the encounter actually takes place, be it in actual facts or in the more conscious dialogue, one needs some root-metaphors in order to articulate the different problems. It is here that some models may prove useful. I shall briefly describe five of them.

2. FIVE MODELS

I repeat that these root-metaphors are only ways to present the problematic of the religious encounter and instruments for expressing different views but not criteria to discriminate between good and bad distinctions, true and false theories, or even authentic and inauthentic religions. This is why they are paradigms. They serve many purposes and certainly too many for those who would like to maintain a particular opinion. This is not only a legitimate wish; it is ultimately a necessity lest we fall prey of sheer chaos, but this is not our concern here. Our models are such precisely because they are polyvalent. They open the dialogue; they do not close it.

a. The Geographical Model: The Ways to the Mountain Peak

It would be hard to argue that human beings are complete and perfect or that they have already fulfilled their destiny. No matter how we express it, we all agree that in some manner or another we have not yet reached the goal, be it God, salvation, annihilation, peace, progress, success, happiness, power, security, and so forth. A way of saying it makes use of a geographical paradigm: we are still pilgrims toward the summit (of life). Ultimately, we do not even know what shape this summit has, whether it is a peak or a plane, whether it is one or many. To be sure, prophets and holy founders, saints and philosophers, mystics and theologians as well as visionaries and charlatans have told us lofty things about those heights. Many speak about it, but their language is not unanimous. Many affirm that behind the snow-clad peaks lies a sunny valley, while others shout that it has been revealed to them that the "summit" lies in the cave of the heart. Some state that the peak is the void, a total abyss of nothingness, or even that all there is is the absurd or the disenchantment that inevitably attends our alienating dreams of a promised Land. Still others claim that there is fullness at the summit, that it is permeated with peace and joy. In any case, however much the religious cartographers may dispute the nature of it, all will admit there is indeed some kind of summit to be reached.

In this context, then, we can consider a religion to be a way that claims to lead to the summit—whether this summit is transcendent or immanent, whether the goal is conquered by individual effort or is received in and enhanced by grace, et cetera.

This summit has many names. Yet no matter how pertinent these names may be, they do not properly describe the actual peak, which is generally considered to be ineffable and inaccessible as long as we are in our present human condition. There are, in fact, many ways claiming to lead to the summit, and all of them are more or less arduous. In other words, the paths are climbs toward one mountain or steps toward one abyss: the mountain inverted.

Elaborating on the metaphor, we may also point out that at the foothills you may not even be aware of the efforts and accomplishments of the other traditions, for many ridges and valleys may separate you from them and prevent you from seeing the trail they have blazed. In the lower ranges the paths are wide apart, while higher up they come closer to each other.

Moreover, although your tradition has marked off a way for you, you still have to follow it on your own. You have to travel on it, and within the larger avenue that has been set out, you somehow have to find or create your own trail. Religion is a very personal concern and thus has an intimate and social dimension.

Furthermore, the geographical model clarifies the fact that if you go on jumping from one way to another you will certainly not reach the goal. You may stop to catch your breath, to enjoy the view, or to harvest a bouquet of wild flowers, but if you reject your calling simply because it is difficult for you and you refuse to climb, you will not reach the top. You have to continue steadfastly on your way.

The way, however, may not conform to your preconceptions and these may have to be abandoned: you have to make your own way. There you may discover hidden paths and shortcuts, as ascetics and guides will tell you. This does not mean that at a certain moment of your pilgrimage you may not discover another trodden path that is more convincing and congenial to you. You may change your way, but nobody can erase your previous pilgrimage. In other words, conversion is a legitimate step when it is not a total rejection of what you have been going through all the way up until then. You can go back at a point where you think you departed from your right path, but even then you cannot begin again as if it were the first step of your journey. Rather, you carry the bundle of your experience with you as you enter into another tradition. You may have discovered that your *dharma* now leads you along a different avenue. Authentic conversion is not a move against your *svadharma*, but rather a movement that tries to regain harmony with your innermost nature.

The changing of ways is no simple affair; it is laden with unforeseen consequences. In spite of yourself, you not only bring all your former equipment over from the other tradition, but you also initiate a complicated process of metabolism. Depending on many factors, some things are discarded and others are assimilated and transformed into the new tradition.

More complex is the case in which wayfarers would like to follow a path different than their own without abandoning the originary one. A new way must be cleared. If successful, this may become a path on which many others may also go. The ways may actually come nearer or extend further when such a passing-over takes place on a sociologically relevant scale.

These considerations lead to a very broad understanding of the word *way*. Each traditional way is then a slope of the mountain on which people find their paths. Valleys may separate the traditional ways at points far away from the peak, but at a certain height two watersheds may meed, and the valleys are left behind. As any mountaineer knows, you need a kind of faith to follow the path, for often the peak remains invisible and ultimately you do not know whether you will have to double back to a safer byway. The trail you have taken may suddenly fall off into sheer space or end abruptly at a granite wall. Nor is this all: Landslides, floods, and even earthquakes may have blocked ancient trails. Indeed, religions change, degenerate, and even die. A jungle of routine and ritualism may have covered up the classical routes, or the weeds of misunderstanding and pride may have chocked off the way of the Golden Age.

This model of the religious quest seems to offer a suitable language to express almost anything about the religious dialogue: that only your way leads to the top; that all the ways may reach the goal; that only some are traversable; that there are meandering trails and dead ends; that at a certain moment no way is of any avail. Another opinion will strike a compromise affirming that the paths exist only on the lower slopes of the climb and that afterward there is no way whatsoever, and so on. It also tells us that, whatever the summit may be, if we destroy all the paths, the summit will collapse. If you erode the slopes, the peak crumbles down. The way is somehow the goal.

The most *jñānic* or gnostic attitudes may tell us that there is no way because "saṁsāra is *nirvāṇa*," or "thou art that" or some similar intuition. The advocates of such ideas, however, cannot deny that the 'no-way' of the realization is also a way to be discovered by the wayfarer.

Moreover, the way must traverse not only the ruggedness of the geographical terrain, but also the psychic topography and inner landscape of the pilgrim, or more simply: The way is only a way if you go through it, if you walk on it and make it your own. We can speak authoritatively only concerning the ways through which we have gone. Yet we must be careful not to limit ourselves to an individualistic interpretation that would rob the metaphor of its flexibility. What may be the proper way for you may not be a true path for me. You may not be able to climb along cracks in the sheer granite walls, while I have an allergy to a path that goes through tropical bushes; you may have vertigo and not tolerate a precipice, while I may get sick from too many curves. I will have to trust you when you say that you will also reach the top safely, although for me your way would not be a 'way' for me.

In our modern technological era there may be people who think that the old ways are well and good for times past but that nowadays we must have new "pontiffs," that is, new bridge builders and a priesthood of professionals who can assist us along the way better than the popes and bonzes of olden times. The "new" or "modern" ways would then be trying to construct the superhighways of a linear morality, a secure and well-measured success, and a well-engineered evolution of human nature. They claim to bridge over the cliffs of ignorance and superstition and to race forward toward the goal in vehicles better designed and equipped than the *mahāyāna* and *hīnayāna* of old. This sometimes shallow interpretation of the model, however, should not be cast aside too quickly, but rather it should be understood in terms of its depth of intuition: that we are not only wayfarers, but also pathfinders and waymakers; that we are the human engineers who construct the roads for a better, more human and thus more divine life—or for worse. This modern spirit has, in fact, historically changed the course of traditional ways such that, while before they were parallel and mutually ignorant, today, willy-nilly they meet and cross. While apparently dealing with only secular pursuits, modern communication systems have actually made a significant contribution to the meeting of religious ways.

Finally, this model may also serve to explain the obvious differences among religions. If one religion *believes* that the summit is a purely transcendent peak that has little in common with our present status, it would consider the way to be one of renouncing anything earthly. If another religion *believes* that the peak is at the very end of the way, it would not ask for an initiation with a leap of faith or a rupture of planes, but rather it would consider the way to be a march through personal effort toward that end. If the peak is inaccessible, grace is needed; if the peak can be seen, intuition is required; if the summit is invisible, faith is indispensable; if the goal is in yourself, interiority is the way; and so forth and so on.

b. The Physical Model: The Rainbow

The different religious traditions of mankind are like the almost infinite number of colors that appear once the divine or simply white light of reality falls on the prism of human experience: it diffracts into innumerable traditions, doctrines and religions. Green is not yellow, hinduism is not buddhism and yet at the fringes one cannot know, except by postulating it artificially, where yellow ends and green begins. Even more, through any particular color, namely religion, one can reach the source of the white light. Any follower of a human tradition is given the possibility of reaching his or her destination, fullness, salvation provided there is a beam of light and not sheer darkness. If two colors mix, they may sire another. Similarly with religious traditions, the meeting of two may give birth to a new one. In point of fact, most of the known religions today are results of such mutual fecundations (aryans-dravidians, jews-greeks, indians-muslims, etc.). Further, it is only from an agreed point of view that we can judge a religion over against another. Regarding social concern, for instance, one tradition may be more fruitful than another, but the latter may be more powerful than the former in securing personal happiness. We may begin the rainbow with the infrared or with the ultraviolet or choose, for instance, 5.000 angstroms as the central point, and so forth. Furthermore, within the green area all will appear under that particular light. A similar object within the red area will look reddish. This model reminds us that the context is paramount in comparing "religious truths." Nor is this all. Just as the color of a body is the only color generally not absorbed by that body, this model would remind us also that a religion similarly absorbs all other colors and hides them in its bosom so that its external color is in truth only its appearance, its message to the outer world, but not the totality of its nature. We come to this realization when we attempt to understand a religion from within. The real body that has received the entire beam of white light keeps for itself all the other colors so that it would not accord with truth to judge a religion only from its outer color. This metaphor can still take more refinements. One particular religion may include only a few beams of light while another may cover a wider aspect of the spectrum. Time and space may (like the principle of Doppler-Fizeau) introduce modifications in the wavelength of a particular tradition so that it changes down the ages or along with the places. What is a christian in the India of the twentieth century may be far different from what was considered such in tenth-century France.

This metaphor does not necessarily imply that all the religions are the same, that there may not be black or colorless spots, that for some particular problems only one particular color may be the appropriate one, and so on. The metaphor, moreover, could still serve to contest the right of something that does not have light in it to be called a religious tradition.

A humanistic critique of traditional religions, for instance, may well call obscurantistic all the religions of the past and deny to them the character of bearing light; only the enlightenment traditions of rationalism, marxism, and humanism, let us say, would come into consideration. I am citing this extreme case in order to clarify the immense variation possible in the use of this root-metaphor. It could even provide an image for the conception of one particular religion considering itself as the white beam and all the others as refractions of that primordial religiousness, or, on the contrary, it may offer an example of how to say that the variety of religions belongs to the beauty and richness of the human situation because it is only the entire rainbow that provides a complete picture of the true religious dimension of Man.

Yet the value of a model comes not only from its possible applicability, but also from its connaturality with the phenomenon under analysis. The physical fact of the rainbow in this case helps us to explain the intricacies of the anthropological phenomenon of religion.

c. The Geometrical Model: The Topological Invariant

If in the first model diffraction is what produces the different lights, or religions, transformation is the cause of the different forms and shapes of geometrical figures—of religions—in our third model.

In and through space and also due to the influence of time, a primordial and original form takes on an almost indefinite number of possible transformations through the twisting of Men, the stretching by history, the bending by natural forces, and so on. Religions appear to be different and even mutually irreconcilable until or unless a topological invariant is found. This invariant does not need to be the same for *all* religions. Some may prefer to hold the theory of families of religions, while others may try to work out the hypothesis that all the different human ways come from a fundamental experience transformed according to laws, which as in any geometrical universe have first to be discovered. Again, others may say that religions are actually different until the corresponding topological transformations have been constructed. The model is polyvalent. Homeomorphism is not the same as analogy: It represents a functional equivalence discovered through a topological transformation. Brahman and God are not merely two analogous names; they are homeomorphic in the sense that each of them stands for something that performs an equivalent function within their respective systems. But this can only be formulated once the homeomorphism of a topological equivalence has been found. Religions that may appear at first sight to be very different from each other may find their connections once the topological transformation is discovered that permits connecting the two traditions under consideration. This model offers a challenge to further study and prevents us from drawing hurried conclusions. A literal use of the topological model would assume not only that all religions are transformations of a primordial experience, intuition, or datum (as would be the case with the Rainbow model), but also that each religious tradition is a dimension of the other, that there is a kind of *circumincessio* or *perichôrêsis* or *pratītyasamutpāda* among all the religious traditions of the world so that mere contiguity models are insufficient to express their relation. Religions do not stand side by side, but they are actually intertwined. Viṣṇu dwells in the heart of Śiva and vice versa. Each religion represents the whole for that particular human group, and in a certain way "is" the religion of the other group, only in a different topological form. Perhaps this may be too optimistic a view, but the model provides also for the necessary cautions or restrictions. One cannot a priori, for instance, formulate this theory, but it may well be a working hypothesis spurring our minds toward some transcendental unity of the religious experience of the human race. It is clear that this model excludes neither a divine factor nor a critical evaluation of the human traditions. Sometimes we may not succeed in finding the corresponding topological equivalence, but sometimes it may also be the case that such a transformation does not exist.

According to this model, then, the comparison among religions would not be the business of finding analogies, which are bound to be always somewhat superficial and need a *primum analogatum* as point of reference (which should already belong to the traditions compared if the comparison is to be fair), but would rather be the business of understanding religions from within and discovering their concrete structures and of finding out their corresponding homeomorphisms. Religious variety would appear here not so much as a bountifully colorful universe as different appearances of an inner structure detectable only in a deeper intuition, be this called mystical or scientific.

Now, the topological laws do not need to be merely of a rational or logical nature, as is the case with geometrical topology. They could as well be historical or sui generis. In a word, the topological model is not only useful for possible doctrinal equivalents; it could also serve to explore other forms of correspondence and equivalence. We may succeed in explaining, for instance, how primitive buddhism was reabsorbed in India through a certain *advaita* by means of finding the proper topological laws of transformation.

d. The Anthropological Model: Language

Whatever theory we may defend regarding the origin and nature of religion, whether it be a divine gift or a human invention or both, the fact remains that it is at least a human reality and as such coextensive with another also at least human reality called language. This model considers each religion as a language. This model has ancient antecedents. To the widespread old belief that there were seventy-two languages, some added the conviction that there were equally seventy-two religions. *"Item dixit"*—say the proceedings of an inquisitorial process of the thirteenth century in Bologna, condemning a Cathar—*"quod sicut sunt LXXII lingue, ita sunt LXXII fides."*

Any religion is complete just as any language is that is capable of expressing everything that it feels the need to express. Any religion is open to growth and evolution as any language is. Both are capable of expressing or adopting new shades of meaning, of shifting idioms or emphases, refining ways of expression, and changing them. When a new need is felt in any religious or linguistic world, there are always means of dealing with that need. Furthermore, although any language is a world in itself, it is not without relations with neighboring languages, borrowing from them and open to mutual influences. Yet each language only takes as much as it can assimilate from a foreign language. Similarly with religions: They influence each other and borrow from one another without losing their identity. In an extreme case a religion, like a language, may disappear entirely. The reasons also seem very similar—conquest, decadence, emigration, and so forth.

From the internal point of view of each language and religion, it makes little sense to say that one language is more perfect than another, for you can in your language (as well as in your religion) say all that you feel you need to say. If you felt the need to say something else or something different, you would say it. If you use only one word for *camel* and hundreds for the different metals, and if another language does just the opposite, it is because you have different patterns of differentiation for camels and metals. It is the same with religions. Yours may have only one word for *wisdom, God, compassion* or *virtue,* and another religion may have scores of them.

The great problem appears when we come to the encounter of languages—and religions. The question here is translation. Religions are equivalent to the same extent that languages are translatable, and they are unique as much as languages are untranslatable. There is the common world of objectifiable objects. They are the objects of empirical or logical verification. This is the realm of terms. Each term is an epistemic sign standing for an empirically or logically verifiable object. The terms *tree, wine, atom, four* can be translated into any given language if we have a method of empirically pointing out a visible thing (tree), a physically recognizable substance (wine), a physicomathematically definable entity (atom), and a logical cipher (four). Each of these cases demands some specific conditions, but we may assume that these conditions can all be empirically or logically verifiable once a certain axiom is accepted. In short, all terms are translatable insofar as a name could easily be invented or adopted even by a language that might lack a particular term (*atom* for instance). Similarly, all religions have a translatable sphere: All refer to the human being, to his well-being, to overcoming the possible obstacles to it, and the like. Religious terms—qua terms—are translatable.

The most important part of a language as well as of a religion, however, is not terms but words, that is, not epistemic signs to orient us in the world of objects but living symbols to allow us to live in the world of Men and Gods. Now, words are not objectifiable. A word is not totally separable from the meaning we give to it, and each of us in fact gives different shades of meaning to the same word. A word reflects a total human experience and cannot be severed from it. A word is not empirically or logically detectable. When we say "justice", *dharma, karuṇā,* we cannot point to an object but have to refer to crystallizations of human experiences that vary with people, places, ages, and so on. We cannot properly speaking translate words. We can only transplant them along with a certain surrounding context that gives them meaning and offers the horizon over against which they can be understood, that is, assimilated within another horizon. Even then the transplanted word, if it survives, will soon extend its roots in the soil and acquire new aspects, connotations, and so forth. Similarly with religions: They are not translatable like terms; only certain transplants are possible under appropriate conditions. There is not an object 'God', 'justice', or 'Brahman', a thing in itself independent of those living words, over against which we may check the correction of the translation. In order to translate them we have to transplant the corresponding worldview that makes those words say what they intend to say. A nonsaying word is like a nonsung song: If the word is not heard as saying what it intends to say, we have not actually translated that word. The translation of religious insights cannot be done unless the insight that has originated that word is also transplanted. Now for this, a mere "sight" from the outside is not sufficient. We may then translate only the outer carcass of a word and not its real meaning. No word can be cut from its speaker if it has to remain an authentic word and not a mere term. The translator has to be also a speaker in that foreign language, in that alien tradition; he has to be a true spokesman for that religion; he has to be, to a certain extent (that I shall not describe further here), convinced of the truth he conveys, converted to the tradition from which he translates. Here I am already in the intrareligious dialogue.

The translator has to speak the "foreign" language as his own. As long as we speak a language translating from another, we shall never speak fluently or even correctly. Only when we speak that language, only when you "speak" that religion as your own will you really be able to be a spokesman for it, a genuine translator. This obviously implies at the same time that you have not forgotten your native tongue, that you are equally capable of expressing yourself in the other linguistic world. It is then that one begins to wonder at the exactness of the translations or, as the expression still goes, at the "fidelity" of many a translation. Are you keeping fidelity to both Brahman and God, *dharma* and religion (or justice, or order?) when you translate in that way; or are you obliged to enlarge, to deepen, and to stretch your own language in order to make place for the insights of the other? This may be the case even with terms that are in part empirically verifiable. Are you so sure that when you translate *gau* with "cow" you are not misleading the modern English reader if you let him believe that you speak merely of a bovine female related perhaps to cowboys but not to the *kāmadhenu*? *Gau* is more than a zoological name, as *sūrya* (sun) is more than a mere name for an astronomical or physical body. *Dhvani* is a reality all poets know.

The linguistic model helps also in the complicated problem of Comparative Religion. Only when we have a common language can we begin to compare, that is, to weigh against a common background. Only then may a mutual understanding take place. This model, moreover, makes it clear that we cannot compare languages (religions) outside language (religion) and that there is no language (religion) except in concrete languages (religions). Comparative religion can only be comparative religions from the standpoint of the concrete religions themselves. This demands an entirely new method from that arising out of the assumption that there is a nonreligious neutral 'reason' entitled to pass comparative judgments in the field of religions.

e. The Mystical Model: Silence

It should not be too quickly retorted that silence cannot be a model because it simply eliminates the problem by not wanting to detect the differences. There is certainly a silence of indifference as well as a silence of skepticism. But there is also a silence that does not deny the word but is aware that the silence is prior to the word and that the word simply words the silence that makes the word possible. The second person of the Trinity, the Logos, came out of the Silence of the first person, some Fathers of the Church used to say.

Mystics of all types and times have privileged this model. They tell us that every word is only a translation. There may be better and worse translations, and we may have lost the original and are bound to struggle with translators, but whenever we forget that the image is not the thing, this model will help us.

The true silence keeps quiet and is put under the test when we become convinced that a particular interpretation is not correct. The temptation is then strong to postulate a "transcendental unity of religions" or an "essential harmony." This may be the case, but the moment that we formulate it we break the silence and with it the unity and the harmony.

Perhaps this model is not a full-fledged model, but only a canvas on which other models can be better situated.

* * * * *

We did not intend a typology of opinions on our problem, but only what we called the rhetoric of the dialogue, that is, the more subjective and human approach to the diversity of religions and ways to deal with the question that is neither a merely psychological perspective nor a purely objective classification.

Our double fivefold description is neither exhaustive, of course, nor mutually exclusive. We find sometimes in the same person the use of more than one model and the adoption of more than one attitude.

2
The Dialogical Dialogue

Tat tvam asi
That are you.
—*Chāndogya Upaniṣad* VI, 8, 7

1. BACKGROUND

THE OVERALL BACKGROUND OF THESE PAGES IS CONSTITUTED by the awareness of the pluralistic and cross-cultural nature of our present-day human situation: Pluralistic because no single culture, model, ideology, religion, or whatnot can any longer raise a convincing claim to be *the* one, unique, or even best system in an absolute sense; cross-cultural because human communities no longer live in isolation, and consequently any human problem today that is not seen in pluri-cultural parameters is already methodologically wrongly put.

The philosophical background of this discussion can be seen in the urge to overcome the unconvincing monistic and dualistic answers to the fundamental problem of the 'One and the Many.' Ultimately I am pleading for an advaitic or nondualistic approach. Its theological horizon is the same philosophical dilemma that takes the form of a God who cannot be totally different from or totally identical with Man and/or World without disappearing. Ultimately, it is a challenge to monotheism and to polytheism alike. At this level atheism belongs morphologically to monotheism. I am here making the plea that God is neither the Other nor the Same but the One: the one pole in a cosmotheandric insight. The cosmotheandric vision sees the entire reality as the interaction of a threefold polarity: cosmic, divine, and human.

The epistemological formulation of the same problematic voices the inadequacy of the subject-object paradigm of knowledge. My contention here is that no knower can be known as knower—it would then become the known—and yet *is*. Being is more than consciousness, although the latter is the manifestation of the former. Both are 'coextensive' from the point of view of consciousness but not necessarily identical.

Its sociological aspect is evident in the apparent aporias that any serious study of comparative civilizations encounters. No religion, system, or tradition is totally self-sufficient. We need each other and yet find our ideas and attitudes mutually incompatible and ourselves often incapable of bridging the gulf between different world views and different basic human attitudes to reality.

The anthropological assumption is that Man is not an individual but a person, that is, a set of relationships of which the I-Thou-It, in all the genders and numbers, is the most fundamental.

With all the qualifications that the foregoing affirmations need, I submit that one of the causes of this present state of affairs lies in the fact that we need a fundamental reflection on method as well as on the nature of pluralism. This study concerns the first issue, although it is intimately bound up with the second.

The immensity of the problem would require a whole treatise. I shall limit myself to describing a possible method to deal with the particular problem of the cross-cultural encounter, on an ultimate level obviously, and to unveil some of its assumptions. Let us begin in medias res.

I have taken as motto the most important of the Upanishadic *mahāvāk ya* or Great Utterances: *tat tvam asi*. This mantra is not just a repetition of the other Great Utterances affirming that *brahman* is the *ātman*, consciousness, and the I. It means properly the discovery of the thou: *brahman* is The

Thou. "That (subject) art thou (predicate)." *Brahman* cannot be the predicate of anything, so the text does not say you are that, that is, *brahman*, but *that* (that is, *brahman*) *are you*. The text does not speak in the third person. It is a dialogue, and thus it does not affirm *brahman* is you, but it reveals to Śvetaketu '*brahman* art you.' Transposing it in the third person, it says that (*brahman*) is a you in you—because *that* (is what) *you are*. But I am not indulging here in vedic hermeneutics. I am only underscoring the fact that besides the *it*, the objective world, and eventually the *I*, the subjective realm, there is also the *thou*, which is neither the objective world of the *it* nor the subjective realm of the ego.

In other words, I am trying to overcome both the Cartesian dualism of the *res cogitans* and the *res extensa*, and the idealistic dichotomy of the *Ich* and the *Nicht-Ich*. In the last instance, I am criticizing any type of dualism without, for that matter, subscribing to any kind of monism. I am submitting that we have also the sphere of the *thou*, which presents an ontonomy irreducible to the spheres of the *I* and the *it*. The *thou* is neither autonomous vis-à-vis the I nor dependent heteronomically on it. It presents a proper ontonomical relation, that is, an internal relation constitutive of its own being. The thou is therefore neither independent of nor dependent on the I, but interrelated. Consciousness is not only I consciousness, but it entails also a thou-consciousness, that is, not my consciousness of you but 'your' consciousness, you as knower, irreducible to what you (and I) know. Because thou-consciousness for you takes the form of I-consciousness, the 'It-Philosophy' has tried to lump all consciousness together and forged the concept of a *Bewusstsein überhaupt*, a general consciousness. Then it has hypostasized it on an absolute subject. Whatever this supreme consciousness may be, it cannot be the sum-total of all I-consciousness because many of those I-consciousnesses are contradictory and irreducible. If at all, it would have to be a supreme *coincidentia oppositorum* or a purely formal consciousness without any content. This conception, be it called God or Brahman or whatever, is what I have designed as monotheism.

Now, coming back to the sublunary world, as the ancients loved to say, in the realm of our human experiences, this implies that in order to have an undistorted vision of reality, we cannot rely exclusively on 'our' consciousness but have somehow to incorporate the consciousness of other people about themselves and the world as well. In order to do this a thematically new method is suggested: the dialogical dialogue. I say "thematically," meaning a conscious reflection on the topic, because the method has been spontaneously employed since many times the dialogue among people is more than 'academic'—and even contemporary anthropology tends to it by stressing participatory approaches and the like.

The perceptive reader will of course discover that the background of the following reflections is also constituted by the contemporary insights of the Sociology of Knowledge (M. Scheler *et al.*), of Hermeneutical Criticism (Gadamer *et al.*), Existential Phenomenology (Strasser *et al.*), Personalism of all sorts (Ebner *et al.*), and Social Theory (Habermas *et al.*), plus the age-old philosophical self-consciousness that goes from Parmenides to Heidegger and from the Upaniṣads to K. C. Bhattacharya, passing through Husserl, Śaṅkara, *et al.*

The relevance of the dialogical dialogue for the Encounter of religious traditions and the so-called Comparative Religion is obvious. I cannot really know—and thus compare—another ultimate system of beliefs unless somehow I share those beliefs, and I cannot do this until I know the holder of those beliefs, the you—not as other (that is, nonego), but as a you. Please note that I speak of beliefs and not just objectified opinions about things.

This much for an overcondensed introduction to the problematic.

2. THESIS

The foundation for the thesis of this chapter rests on the assumption that the ultimate nature of reality does not have to be dialectical. If we postulate it to be so, we do it by the already dialectical axiom that affirms reality to be solely or ultimately dialectical. Reality has no foundation other than itself, and if we assume it to be dialectical we are already postulating what reality has to be and imprisoning it in the dialectical frame, large and flexible as one may conceive this latter to be. The postulate of the dialectical nature of reality is an extrapolation of the conviction about the dialectical nature of the mind; it subordinates reality to mind.

My thesis is that the dialogical dialogue is not a modification of the dialectical method or a substitution for it. It is a method that both limits the field of dialectics and complements it. It *limits* dialectics, insofar as it prevents dialectics from becoming logical monism, by putting forward another method that does not assume the exclusively dialectical nature of reality. It *complements* dialectics by the same token. It is not a direct critique of dialectics, but only a guard against dialectical totalitarianism.

The thesis says, further, that the dialogical dialogue is the proper, although not exclusive, method for what I have called *'diatopical'* hermeneutics. By diatopical hermeneutics I understand a hermeneutic that is more than the purely morphological (drawing from the already known deposit of a particular tradition) and the merely diachronical one (when we have to bridge a temporal gap in order to arrive at a legitimate interpretation). It is a hermeneutic dealing with understanding the contents of diverse cultures that do not have cultural or direct historical links with one another. They belong to different loci, *topoi*, so that before anything else we have to forge the tools of understanding in the encounter itself, for we cannot—should not—assume a priori a common language. The privileged place of this hermeneutic is obviously the encounter of religious traditions. A christian cannot assume at the outset that he knows what a buddhist means when speaking about *nirvāṇa* and *anātman*, just as a buddhist cannot immediately be expected to understand what a christian means by God and Christ before they have encountered not just the concepts but their living contexts, which include different ways at looking at reality: They have to encounter each other before any meeting of doctrines. This is what the dialogical dialogue purports to be: the method for the encounter of persons and not just individuals, on the one hand, or mere doctrines on the other.

3. DIALOGUE AND DIALECTICS

Let me emphatically assert that this essay is neither an attack on dialectics nor a critique of rationality. Dialectics, in spite of its many meanings, stands for the dignity of the human logos endowed with the extraordinary prerogative of discriminating between truth and error by means of thinking: *ars iudicandi,* said the Scholastics, condensing Cicero's definition of dialectics as *veri et falsi iudicandi scientia.* It is of course a matter of philosophical dispute where to locate this human power, its name and nature; at any rate we may accept the well-known Hegelian description of dialectics as: *die wissenschaftliche Anwendung der in der Natur des Denkens liegenden Gesetzmässigkeit* (the scientific application of the inner structure [the internal law, the law-governedness] inherent in the nature of thinking).

We could, of course, try to harmonize most of the thinkers who have in the past used this word (in the present, the inflation makes any overview almost impossible) and define it as διαλεκτικὴ τεχνή or as *ars scientiaque disputandi,* that is, the craft of human verbal intercourse. In this definition we would embrace Plato's 'conversation' in questions and answers, as well as Aristotle's conception of reasoning on probable opinions, Kant's logic of appearances and, through Hegel's dictum that *das Selbstbewusstsein wesentliches Moment des Wahren ist* ("self-consciousness is an essential moment of truth"), the marxist's interpretation of dialectics as the method of true thinking because it constitutes the expression of the dynamic coherence of otherwise contradictory historical reality. In this wider sense the dialogical dialogue is still dialogue and thus dialectical or conversational. But we may legitimately assume that when nowadays people use the word *dialectic* they imply that tight relationship between thinking and being about which I shall later express my critical doubts. They mean also a technique which empowers one to pass judgments on other people's opinions and not a mere art of conversation. In this sense the dialogical dialogue lies outside the sphere of dialectics. *Dia-logical* here would stand for piercing, going through the logical and overcoming—not denying—it. The dialogical dialogue is in its proper place when dealing with personal, cross-cultural, and pluralistic problems. In all three cases we deal with situations not totally reducible to the logos.

Personal problems are those in which the complexity of the whole human person is at stake and not merely mental quandaries or, for that matter, any other partial queries. A personal problem is not a sheer technical puzzle of how to reestablish the proper functioning of the human organism. The human being is certainly a rational animal and rationality may be its most precious gift, but the realm of reason does not exhaust the human field. It is not by dialectically convincing the patients that the psychotherapist will cure them. It is not by proving one side to be right that a war can be avoided. There is no dialectical proof for love. Not less but something more is required.

A *cross-cultural* problem arises from the encounter of two cultures, for example, when somebody insists that the earth is a living being and should be treated as such against a technological view of the planet. It cannot be solved dialectically. We should avoid using the word *cross-cultural* when we mean only the study of another culture different from our own but still with the categories of the latter. A cross-cultural approach to Asia, for instance, does not mean 'orientalism' in the Victorian sense of the word. Cross-cultural studies deal with the very perspective in which the 'problem' is approached. They reformulate the very problem by using categories derived from the two cultures concerned. Scholastically speaking, we may say that cross-cultural studies are not characterized by their 'material object' (say, India or hinduism from a western stance), but by their 'formal object' (say, the scale of values, perspectives, views, and categories we apply to apprehend the very 'problem'). I am saying here that dialectics are not cross-cultural enough. Dialectics are a knowledge with an 'interest' arising from a particular worldview, and the very interest in universalizing the dialectical method—especially the historical dialectics—reinforces our affirmation. We need another method for cross-cultural studies—before any discussion in the dialectical arena.

4. DIALECTICAL DIALOGUE

The dialectical dialogue supposes that we are rational beings and that our knowledge is governed above all by the principle of noncontradiction. You and I admit it as a given, and if you lead me into contradiction I will either have to give up my opinion or attempt to overcome the impasse. We present our respective points of view to the Tribunal of Reason, in spite of the variety of interpretations that we may hold even of the nature of reason. The dialectical dialogue trusts Reason and in a way the reasonableness of the other—or of the whole historical process. It admits, further, that none of us exhausts the knowledge of the data. On this basis we engage in dialogue. If we refuse the dialogue it is because, even without saying it, we assume that someone is motivated by ill will and not ready to abide by the fair play of dialectics or else is mentally weak, fears defeat, or the like. It is obvious that there are fields proper to the dialectical dialogue, and even that it can never be bypassed. If we deny reason or reasonableness, we make impossible any type of dialogue.

As we shall expound later again, the dialectical dialogue is a necessary intermediary in the communication between human beings. Dialectics have an irreplaceable mediating function at the human level. The dialectical dialogue cannot be brushed away in any truly human exchange. We have the need to judge and to discriminate for ourselves—not necessarily for others—between right and wrong. It would amount to falling into sheer irrationalism to ignore this essential role of dialectics.

5. DIALOGICAL DIALOGUE

The dialectical dialogue is a dialogue about objects that, interestingly enough, the English language calls 'subject matters'. The dialogical dialogue, on the other hand, is a dialogue among subjects aiming at being a dialogue about subjects. They want to dialogue not about something, but about themselves: They dialogue themselves. In short, if all thinking is dialogue, not all dialogue is dialogical. The dialogical dialogue is not so much about opinions (the famous *endoxa*, ἔνδοξα of Aristotle about which dialectics deal) as about those who have such opinions, and eventually not about you, but about me to you. To dialogue about opinions, doctrines, views, the dialectical dialogue is indispensable. In the dialogical dialogue the partner is not an object or a subject merely putting forth some objective thoughts to be discussed, but a you, a real you and not an it. I must deal with you and not merely with your thought, and of course, vice versa, You yourself are a source of understanding.

Now, two persons cannot talk each other; they have to talk *to* each other. This means that the talk has to be mediated by something else. The medium is a language, and if there is language there is thought. They cannot dialogue themselves; they need the mediation of language. In any dialogue there is something outside of and in a way superior to the partners that link them together. They have to be speaking about something and this something has an inner structure that the participants have to respect and acknowledge. But this something is only a mediator conveying to each of them not just 'thoughts', that is, objectifiable ideas, but thematically a part of themselves. In other words, this something is not made independent, 'objective', but is seen in its peculiar *dialogical intentionality.*

In order to describe the characteristics of this dialogical dialogue, we have been contrasting it with the dialectical one. It should be made clear that the relation between the two is not dialectical; they are two intertwined moments of the dialogical character of the human being. There is no pure dialectical dialogue. When two persons enter into dialogue, in spite of all the efforts to keep the 'personal' to a bare minimum, it emerges all along. We never have an encounter of pure ideas. We always have an encounter of two (or more) persons. This aspect of the human being often emerges conspicuously in the actual praxis of the dialectical dialogue, in which the partners, forgetting that they are supposed to be thinking beings, indulge in getting involved in quite different but also real aspects of human life. To discard those aspects as "sentimental" or as "passions" obscuring the work of Reason misses the point. Sentiments also belong to the human being. There are, further, cases in which what is at issue are not emotional ingredients but fundamental options stemming from different self-understandings. But there is much more than this. There is no pure *theory.* It is always 'tinged' with interests and connected with the milieu that accepts it as theory.

Similarly, there is no dialogical dialogue alone. Two subjects can only enter into dialogue if they 'talk' about something, even if they are interested in knowing each other and in wanting to know themselves better by means of the mirror-effect on the other. The dialogical dialogue is not a mute act of love. It is a total human encounter, and thus it has an important intellectual component. It is precisely the importance of the very subject matter of the dialogue that unveils the depths of the respective personalities and leads to the dialogical dialogue proper.

This emphasizes a fact that is often only latent in the merely dialectical dialogue: the will to dialogue. This will is here paramount. It is not that if I do not will to enter into dialogue I keep my mouth shut. It is that if I do not have that will even if I speak with my partner I will not enter into any dialogical dialogue. Here no pretense would do. The dialectical dialogue can be an instrument to power and can be a means to the will to power. This is not the case with the dialogical dialogue. It is for this reason that any further intention, the intention, for example, to convert, to dominate, or even to know the other for ulterior motives, destroys the dialogical dialogue.

The trusting in the other, considering the other a true source of understanding and knowledge, the listening attitude toward my partner, the common search for truth (without assuming that we already know what words mean to each of us), the acceptance of the risk of being defeated, converted, or simply upset and left without a north—these are not pragmatic devices to enable us to live in peaceful coexistence because the other is already too powerful or vociferous and cannot be silenced. It is not because reason has failed us or that humankind has suddenly experienced a disenchantment with the idea of a possible *pax mundialis* as it is traditionally expressed in the models of One God, One Church, One Empire, One Religion, One Civilization, and now One Technology. The justification of the dialogical dialogue lies much deeper; it is to be found in the very nature of the real, namely in the fact that reality is not wholly objectifiable, ultimately because I myself, a subject, am also a part of it, am *in* it, and cannot extricate myself from it. The dialogical dialogue assumes a radical dynamism of reality, namely that reality is not given once and for all, but is real precisely in the fact that it is continually creating itself—and not just unfolding from already existing premises or starting points.

This is certainly what the modern understanding of dialectics also espouses: Reality is in a state of constant flux, everything depends on everything else, and immutability is not a feature of reality. Still more: Modern dialectics accept the changing nature of reality in such a way that change is made imperative. Change is not contingent but necessary, and it brings about qualitative leaps in the order of things. The overcoming of internal contradictions belongs to the very nature of reality. All this is dialectics. But there is one thing that dialectics cannot give up: the pliability of reality to the dialectical laws of thinking. It is here that the ultimate character of the dialogical dialogue appears clearly, as we shall see in a moment.

From what has been said so far, we may gather the impression that the dialogical dialogue is inbuilt in any authentic and deep dialogue. This is certainly so, but the evolution of human culture, especially in the West, has given predominance to the dialectical aspect of the dialogue, and the dialogical one has been relegated to playing second fiddle. We would like now to unearth some of the assumptions underlying this dialogue. We will then better see its revolutionary character. It challenges, in point of fact, many of the commonly accepted foundations of modern culture. To restore or install the dialogical dialogue in human relations among individuals, families, groups, societies, nations, and cultures may be one of the most urgent things to do in our times threatened by a fragmentation of interests that threatens all life on the planet. In point of fact, one feature of contemporary western culture—mainly subcultures—is the praxis of a certain approach to the dialogical dialogue in the form of social work and psychotherapies. Yet in many cases, the lack of the 'dialogical intentionality' makes such methods ineffective.

6. THINKING AND BEING

The dialogical dialogue assumes, we said, that nobody can predict or fathom the dynamism of being because this latter is not mere evolution but also creativity. We could say, paraphrasing an Upaniṣad, that even the mind has to recoil and stand back. Science is that astonishing feat made possible because our thinking can foretell how beings are going to behave. This is an incontrovertible fact. But nothing stands in the way of reality expressing itself freely in ways not predictable by thinking of any kind. The spontaneity and creativity of Nature may be hidden in its very recesses, perhaps at the origins of time and at the infra-atomic levels, as modern science begins to surmise, but certainly (the human) being possesses a factor of creativity and spontaneity that cannot be encapsulated in any a priori scheme. This creativity constitutes the locus of the dialogical dialogue. To sum up: Dialectics, in one way or another, deals with the power of our mind but assumes a peculiar relation between thinking and being.

Here comes the great divide. It is one thing to assert that thinking tells us what being is and another thing to make being utterly dependent on thinking. In other words, the justification of dialectics does not depend on the often uncritically accepted hypothesis that the nature of reality is dialectical. Reality certainly has a dialectical aspect, but this aspect does not have to be all of the real. It is in this hiatus between thinking and being that the dialogical dialogue finds its *ultimate* justification. There are human situations that do not necessarily fall under the jurisdiction of the dialectical dialogue because reality does not have to be exhaustively dialectical. The laws of thought are laws of being, and this makes science possible, but not necessarily vice versa. Rather, being does not have to have—or always follow—laws, however useful such a hypothesis may be. Being is not exclusively restricted to be what thinking postulates. This makes ontic freedom possible and constitutes the ultimate *onto*-logical problem: The *logos* of the *on* is only the *on* of the *logos,* but this latter is not identical with the former. The *on* is 'bigger' than the *logos.* The *logos* may be coextensive with the *on,* but still there 'is' the *pneuma* 'between', and 'where Spirit, freedom'. And where there is freedom, thought cannot dictate, foresee, or even necessarily follow the 'expansion', 'explosion', life of Being. We recall that Plato believed ideas have a life of their own.

"Being is said in many ways:" τὸ ὄν πολλαχῶς λέγεται is the famous sentence of Aristotle. But being 'is' also unsaid, at least inasmuch as it has not yet been said. Further, we cannot think how being will speak, that is, will say itself. Yet this unsaid accompanies being. This silent companion may not be in principle unspeakable, but it is actually unspoken. Real silence is not repression of the word and incapacity to think, but absence of the word and transcending of thought.

The dialogical dialogue makes room for this sovereign freedom of being to speak new languages—or languages unknown to the other.

Be this as it may, even without this ultimate foundation, there is place for the dialogical dialogue.

7. SUBJECT AND OBJECT

The most immediate assumption of the dialogical dialogue is that the other is not just an other (*alius*) and much less an object of my knowledge (*aliud*), but another self (*alter*) who is a source of self-understanding, and also of understanding, not necessarily reducible to my own.

Another way of putting it: Reality is not totally objectifiable. The dialectical dialogue takes place in the sphere of the objectifiable reality. We discuss, agree, or disagree on objective grounds, following objective rules. Something is objectifiable when it is in principle conceptualizable. It can then be an object of some thought. What is objectifiable is the conceptual aspect of reality apprehended as such by the subject. But this apparently leaves the subject out of it.

Anything we say about an objective state of affairs is an abstraction. It abstracts from the subject and ignores its influence on the object. It is like freezing the flow of the real. This freezing may well be necessary for a moment in order more easily to apprehend something, but it can become a trap we fall into the moment we forget that it is only a device, and a provisional one, a scaffold we use to reach outside ourselves and grasp something. In other words, the trap is to mistake the objective idea for the real, the concept for the thing—eventually identifying the two. In this setting the others are able only somewhat to qualify or correct my assertions, but certainly not to convert me radically, that is, to throw me out of the fortress of my 'own' private world. From here to an ideology of power there is only a short way to go.

The dialogical dialogue, on the other hand, considers the other as another subject, that is, as another source of (self-)understanding. The others as subjects do not have to be necessarily reduced to an ultimately unique source. This is the question of pluralism (that we said we were leaving aside) and its connection with monotheism: the different subjects participating, each in their own way, from the one single Source of intelligence and intelligibility.

The dialogical dialogue is not concerned so much about opinions as about the different viewpoints from which the respective opinions are arrived at. Now, to deal with a perspective means to deal with very fundamental springs in the knowing subject. A new epistemology is required here. Just as any knowledge of an object requires a certain connaturality and identification with the object to be known, any knowledge of the subject necessitates also a similar identification. This is what has led me to formulate the principle of 'Understanding as Convincement'. We cannot understand a person's ultimate convictions unless we somehow share them.

8. I AND THOU

This is not the place to describe the rich evolution of the idea of dialectics. Suffice it to say that it was probably F. H. Jacobi who first saw, in the post-cartesian age, the implicit solipsism of any idealism (including Kant's) and began to develop the idea of a dialogical thinking transcending the constriction of objective dialectics. But it was Feuerbach criticizing Hegel who tried to develop a dialogical dialectic that is a forerunner of the dialogical thinkers of the beginning of this century, Buber, Rosenzweig, and Ebner. Says Feuerbach: "Die wahre Dialektik ist kein Monolog des einsamen Denkers mit sich selbst, sie ist ein Dialog zwischen Ich und Du." (The true dialectic is not a monologue of the individual thinker with himself, but a dialogue between I and Thou.)

Yet, without now entering into a detailed analysis of those predecessors, I may add that the dialogical dialogue I am espousing claims to transcend the realm of dialectics by realizing that the relation I/Thou is irreducible to any relation I/It or I/Non-I, and thus equally ultimate.

A certain type of philosophy, which could be designated broadly as idealism, has potentiated the knowledge of all potential subjects and called it the ultimate or true I as the bearer of all knowledge, as absolute consciousness. Over against this I there remains only the Non-I, be it called world, matter, extension, evil, illusion, appearance, or whatever.

Another type of philosophy, which could broadly be called sociology of knowledge, has stressed the fact of the dependency of the thinking individual on both collectivity and environment. Any individual's thinking expresses only what is thinkable within the community in which that individual thinks, and one's personal contribution makes sense only within the larger context of the community. Furthermore, one's thinking is also a part of human thinking and not only a disconnected heap of human thoughts.

In the first case we have the ultimate dialectical opposition between the I and the Non-I. The individual is part of that I, and when in dialogue with other egos it has only to deepen its participation in the absolute consciousness. The other as subject is invited to do the same; as object it belongs to the sphere of the Non-I.

In the second case the individual's thinking is situated vis-à-vis the collectivity, of which it is also a part. The others are members of the same or a different community sharing in the same or another *Zeitgeist*, as it were.

In both cases the dialogue with the other is directed toward the source of our understanding of reality by means of a sharing in either an absolute consciousness or a collective consciousness of a group in space and time, or even the entire humanity.

This may be true, but there is still more to it. When the individual thinks, he does not think individualistically; he does not think out of himself alone, nor only in contemplation of God or intercourse with the world, that is, with the object of his thinking (his thought), but he thinks already in conformity, harmony with, and/or reaction to, stimulated by, and in dialogue with, other people. Thinking is not an individualistic process, but an act of language.

But language is primarily neither a private activity nor a mystical act in connection with Consciousness or Humanity. It is an exchange with someone in front of us and at our level. It is fundamentally a dialogical activity. What the two just-mentioned considerations have overlooked is precisely that our first verbal relationship is not dialectical but dialogical. We begin by listening, learning, assimilating, comparing, and the like. We are not confronting a nonego but a thou with whom we have a common language or with whom we strive to have one.

In order to think, we cannot succeed alone. We need dialogue with the *thou*. In point of fact, the *I* can only express 'itself' in intercourse with the *thou* or with the *it*. We need the living dialogue because the "I love," "I will," and even "I think" acquires its full meaning only in confrontation with what a 'you' loves, wills, and thinks. This amounts to saying that thinking is only possible within one—our—world, and thus one language, our language.

I am not excluding the dialogue with the it, that is, with things. This is one of the fascinations of Science, and I am even prepared to reinstate animism in the traditional sense of the *anima mundi* and the belief that in one way or another everything is alive, conscious of the fact that this position introduces a revolution in Science: Not only does physics become biology, but science itself becomes dialogical. But in the human dialogue with things, in spite of the fact that things react, offer resistance, are not pliable to the wishes of the human intellect, and in a certain way respond to the human dialogue, they do not have the same interiority and consciousness as human beings. In brief, for the full development of human thinking, even when thinking about things, human dialogue is imperative.

The dialogical dialogue takes you my partner as seriously as myself and by this very fact wakes me up from the slumber of solipsistic speculations, or the dreaming fantasies of a docile partner. We encounter the hard reality of an opposition, another will, another source of opinions, perspectives. The dialogue maintains the constitutive polarity of reality that cannot be split into subject and object without the previous awareness of different subjects speaking. There is not only a subject and an object, but also a subject and another subject, although mediated by an object. This is even inbuilt in language itself. The I and thou statements can never set the speaking subject aside; they cannot be substantives in the sense of being reified, cut off from the I and the thou and made into eternal, immutable 'truths'. In the dialogue we are reminded constantly of our temporality, our contingency, our own constitutive limitations. Humility is not primarily a moral virtue but an ontological one; it is the awareness of the place of my ego, the truthfulness of accepting my real situation, namely, that I am a situated being, a vision's angle on the real, an existence.

As already indicated, the rationale for the dialogical dialogue is that the *thou* has a proper and inalienable ontonomy. The thou is a source of self-understanding that I cannot assimilate from my own perspective alone. It is not as if we all would see 'the same thing' but from a different vantage point. This may be true, but the dialogical dialogue is not just the locus for perspectivism. It does not assume a 'thing in itself', the Elephant in the dark room of the Indian story (one describing 'reality' as a shaft, the other as a pillar, the third as a winnowing fan, and so on). Nor does it assume a mere atomistic view, as if each human being were an independent monad without windows. It assumes, on the contrary, that we all share in a reality that does not exist independently and outside our own sharing in it, and yet without exhausting it. Our participation is always partial, and reality is more than just the sum total of its parts.

9. MYTH AND LOGOS

To be sure, many things happen in the dialectical dialogue: There are winners and losers, some conclusions are arrived at, some new light is shed on the subject matter, new distinctions are made, and so on. Besides and above those things the dialogical dialogue changes the partners themselves in unexpected ways and may open new vistas not logically implied in the premises. The very 'rules' of this dialogue are not fixed a priori; they emerge out of the dialogue itself. The dialogue is not a 'duologue', but a going through the logos: *dia ton logon*, διὰ τὸν λόγον, beyond the logos-structure of reality. It pierces the logos and uncovers the respective myths of the partners. In the dialogical dialogue, we are vulnerable because we allow ourselves to be 'seen' by our partner, and vice versa. It is the other who discovers my myth, what I take for granted, my horizon of intelligibility, the convictions of which lie at the source of my expressed beliefs. It is the other who will detect the hidden reasons for my choice of words, metaphors, and ways of thinking. It is the other who will interpret my silences and omissions in (for me) unsuspected ways.

Now, in order to allow this to happen we need to unearth our presuppositions. But this we cannot do alone. We need the other. We are more or less conscious of our assumptions, that is, of the axioms or convictions that we put at the starting point and use as foundation of our views. But those very assumptions themselves rest on underlying 'pre-sub-positions' that for us 'go without saying' and are 'taken for granted.' But this does not need to be the case for our partner, and he will point them out to us and bring them to the forum of analysis and discussion. We may then either discard them or convert them into conscious assumptions as bases for further thinking.

The dialogical dialogue challenges us on a much deeper level than the dialectical one. With the dialectical dialogue we are unable to explore realms of human experience, spheres of reality, or aspects of being that belong to the first and second persons, that is, to the '*am*' and '*art*' aspects of reality. In other words, with the dialectical dialogue we can only reach the '*it is*' aspect of the real and cannot be in full communication with other subjects and their most intimate convictions. With the dialectical dialogue, we may discuss religious doctrines once we have clarified the context, but we need the dialogical dialogue to discuss beliefs as those conscious attitudes we have in face of the ultimate issues of our existence and life.

In the dialogical dialogue, I trust the other not out of an ethical principle (because it is good) or an epistemological one (because I recognize that it is intelligent to do so), but because I have discovered (experienced) the '*thou*' as the counterpart of the I, as belonging *to* the I (and not as not-I). I trust the partner's understanding and self-understanding because I do not start out by putting my ego as the foundation of everything. It is not that I do not examine my partner's credentials (he could be wicked or a fool), not that I fall into irrationalism (or any type of sentimentalism), giving up my stance, but that I find in his actual presence something irreducible to my ego and yet not belonging to a nonego: I discover the thou as part of a Self that is as much mine as his—or to be more precise, that is as little my property as his.

Now, this discovery of the *ātman*, the human nature, a common essence or divine undercurrent, is not, properly speaking, *my* discovery of *it*, but my discovery of *me*, the discovery of myself as *me*—and not as I: '*Me-consciousness.*'

Further, this dawning of me-consciousness cannot occur without the 'thou' spurring it on, and ultimately the real or ultimate I (*aham*) performing it. Leaving aside now the awareness of the transcendent-immanent I, the fact still remains that without a 'thou' calling and challenging me, my 'me-consciousness' would not emerge. In the dialogical dialogue my partner is not the *other* (it is not he/she, and much less it), but the thou. The thou is neither the other nor the nonego. The thou is the very thou of the I in the sense of the subjective genitive.

It is the cross-cultural challenge of our times that unless the barbarian, the mleccha, goy, infidel, nigger, kafir, foreigner, and stranger are invited to be my thou, beyond those of my own clan, tribe, race, church, or ideology, there is not much hope left for the planet.

This on a world-scale is a *novum*, but an indispensable element for a present-day civilization worthy of humanity. We have mentioned already the importance of the dialogical dialogue for the Encounter of Religions. It is, I submit, the neglect of this method and the application of a predominantly dialectical dialogue among religious traditions that is at the root of so many misunderstandings and enmities among the followers of so many religions. The lack of proper understanding among religions is not so much matter of doctrinal differences—these exist also among schools of the same religion—but of existential attitudes—down often to economic, administrative, and political reasons.

And so, we close the circle. We began by saying that true dialogue is a dialogue among human beings and have underscored that a person is more than a thinking subject; persons are fields of interaction where the real has been woven or striped by means of all the complexity of reality; they are knots in the continuous weaving of the net of reality.

* * * * *

Millennia ago, Chuang Tsu said:

> Assume you and I argue. If you win and I lose, are you right and I wrong? If I win and you lose, am I right and you wrong? Are we both partially right and wrong? Are we both right or both wrong? If you and I cannot see the truth, other people will find it harder.
>
> Whom shall we ask to be the judge? Someone who agrees with you? If he agrees with you how can he be a fair judge? Shall I ask someone who agrees with me? If he does, how can he be a fair judge? Shall I ask

someone who agrees with both of us? If he already agrees with both of us, how can he be a fair judge? If you and I and other cannot decide, shall we wait for still another?

Since the standard of judging right or wrong depends on the changing relative phenomena, then there is fundamentally no standard at all.

Seeing everything in relation to the natural cosmic perspective, argument stops, right and wrong cease to be. We are then free and at ease.

What do I mean by "seeing everything in relation to the natural cosmic perspective, then argument stops"? This is to say that 'right' *can be said* to be 'wrong', 'being', 'non-being'. If something is really right, it naturally has its distinction from wrong. There is no need for argument. Being is naturally distinguished from non-being. There is no need for argument either. Forget all about differentiation between life and death, right and wrong. Be free. Live and play with the infinite.*

*On the basis the published version of G.-F. Fend and J. English, retranslated by Agnes Lee, to whom thanks are expressed.

3

Faith and Belief:
A Multireligious Experience

te 'pi mām eva, . . . yajanti
Me they also worship.
—BG IX, 23

Whoever wishes to care for me,
let him look after the sick ones.
—*Vinayapiṭaka* I, 302

ἐμοὶ ἐποιήσατε
mihi fecistis
you did it unto me.
—Mt. XXV:40

1. INTRODUCTION

T HE DISTINCTION BETWEEN FAITH AND BELIEF, ALONG WITH THE
   thesis that faith is a constitutive human dimension, represents more
than just an intellectual venture. It is equally an existential adventure: a
human pilgrimage within religious traditions divided by multisecular
walls of history, philosophies, theologies, and prejudices. It has been my
karma to undergo such experiences without artificially or even reflec-
tively preparing them. A decade ago, after fifteen years' absence from the
European literary scene, the plainest and yet the most searching question
to ask me was: How have I fared? Although my human pilgrimage was
not yet finished, I used to give a straightforward—obviously incomplete—answer: I 'left' as a christian, I 'found' myself a hindu, and I
'return' a buddhist, without having ceased to be a christian. Some people
nevertheless wonder whether such an attitude is objectively tenable or
even intelligible. Here is a reply in outline that I hope will also throw
some light on the spiritual condition of humankind today—even if it
belongs to my historical past.

2. ECUMENISM TODAY

In ancient Greece, *oikumene* referred to household management. When the
domestic sense broadened the word came to mean the world, but still
within a rather narrow compass—just as when someone says "every-
body" has left Madrid for August vacation, although the only water most
of the people ever see is the trickle in their own channeled River Man-
zanares. Our age prides itself on its ecumenical spirit and has indeed risen
above the clan mentality far enough to acknowledge the right of other
clans to exist, whether they call themselves philosophical systems, religious beliefs, races, or nations. But for all their importance, these ecu-
menisms generally remain very restricted, still far removed from an
ecumenical ecumenism that means more than the mere notion that people
everywhere are human or that my own views and judgments can be
exported quite safely to other countries.

   The great temptation for ecumenism is to extrapolate—to use a native
growth beyond the bounds of its native soil. We have seen what comes of
exporting European and American democracy; we know that the baffling
population explosion over much of the world's surface comes of exporting antibiotics, DDT, and the like. No one-way movement—certainly not

exporting a Gospel—can solve our present problems. I do not for a moment suggest that there be no crossing of borders. I am only saying that most solutions to our problems remain terribly provincial; we do not yet have categories adequate to the exigencies of our *kairos*.

3. THE PROVINCE AND THE PARISH

The confrontation of religions provides an instructive instance of what I am trying to say. Western culture constructs a philosophy or theology of religion and considers it universal. To be more precise, it dashes off judeo-graeco-modern categories and with these attempts to lay hold of religious, cultural, and philosophical phenomena lying many a mile beyond the remotest colony (as it is called), the farthest outpost of its *oikumene*. Thus Asia, for example, compelled to speak in some european language, will have to say 'way' instead of *tao*, 'God' instead of *Brahman* and 'soul' instead of *ātman;* it must translate *dharma* as 'justice', *ch'an* as 'meditation', and so forth. But the problem lies even deeper than the difficulty of suitably translating ideas belonging to other cultural contexts. The problem cannot be "computerized," so to speak, because it involves the very laws that govern the working of our minds—and of computers to boot.

This "neocolonialistic" situation prompts me to observe that while the *province* may betoken narrowness of mind bordering on myopia and may lead to fanaticism and intolerance, the *parish* might connote safeguarding a particular reality, a human scale of things, organic and personal life. The parish is by its very nature a miniature universe quantitatively speaking but is also the entire universe speaking qualitatively (although symbolically). Nevertheless, from the steeple of the parish church many other steeples can be seen. A theological hermeneutic of this symbol tells us that the parish will be whole only when the Pantocrator, the Lord of all the universe, is at its center and there holds communion (this is the right word) with the whole world. Wisdom reaches its pinnacle in a happy commingling of universal and concrete, intellectual and vital, masculine and feminine, divine and human—in short, in cosmotheandric experience. 'Ecumenical ecumenism', a phrase I diffidently put forward some years ago and that now seems to be sweeping the board, might well express this blend of household hearth and universal humanness. The parish lived in all its depth and scope stands for the same thing: homey, down-to-earth, regional things; it means dialect, personal roots, personalizing forms, and at the same time an awareness that we all draw nourishment from a common sap, that one sky arches over us all, that a single mother earth sustains us all.[1] Ecumenical ecumenism does not mean cloudy universalism or indiscriminate syncretism; or a narrow, crude particularism or barren, fanatical individualism. Instead it attempts a happy blending—which I would make bold to call androgynous before calling it theandric—of these two poles, the universal and the concrete, which set up the tension in every creature. In other words, the identity our age so frantically seeks is not individuality (which ends in solipsism) nor generality (which ends in alienation), but the awareness of that constitutive relativity that makes of us but connections in the mysterious warp and woof of being. But I should not go on cheering *pro domo mea* when I am saying my house is the cottage of mankind.

4. AN OBJECTIFIED AUTOBIOGRAPHICAL FRAGMENT

Before embarking on a clearer, more scholarly treatment of the subject, I should like to present it in a personal way, psychological if you will— although not strictly autobiographical.

Here I am a person brought up in the strictest orthodoxy, who has lived as well in a milieu that is 'microdox' from every point of view. It will not do to say now that if I managed to survive, it was thanks to seeds of true life sown even before I had reached the age of reason. This person goes forth, forsaking the land of Ur, to dwell in the land of "Men" (indeed he knew it before, but not through experience, not in his flesh like Job). Instantly he finds himself confronted by a dilemma: Either he must condemn everything around him as error and sin, or he must throw overboard the exclusivistic and monopolistic notions he has been told embody truth—truth that must be simple and unique, revealed once and for all, that speaks through infallible organs, and so on. None of the answers people give to this dilemma satisfy him. The eclectic answer flouts logic and sometimes common sense as well. He cannot make do with the 'orthodox' answer that merely concocts casuistic shifts so that some nook is left for those who profess error through no fault of their own; it does not convince him either as a whole or in its details. So he overcomes the temptation of *relativism* by acknowledging *relativity*. Instead of everything falling into an agnostic or indifferent relativism, everything is wrapped in an utter relativity of radical interdependence because every being is a function in the hierarchical order of beings and has its own place in the dynamism of history, a place not incidental to the thing but actually making the thing what it is.

But the personal problem went deeper still. It involved more than rising above provincialism or acknowledging that today philosophy must recognize cultural differences and account for Man's pluralism. One had to safeguard the parish, uphold one's identity, live by one's faith and yet not cut oneself from others, not look on oneself as a special, privileged being. Can this man keep his feet firmly planted on the ground—on his native soil—while his arms embrace the most distant heavens? Indeed, the problem was trying to live one's faith without an exclusivity that appears outrageously unjust and false even when decked out in notions of grace, election, or what have you. In other words, the whole idea of belonging to a chosen people, of practicing the true religion, of being a privileged creature, struck me not as a grace but a disgrace. Not that I felt myself unworthy, but I thought it would ill become me to discriminate in such a fashion and I thought it would ill become God to do so. I am well aware of the innumerable theoretical ways to get around the objection. I do not claim that this idea runs counter to God's goodness or justice, which presumably is not affected by our revulsion; I contend only that this idea contravenes the freedom and joy I would look for in a belief that enables the human being to grow to full stature. It is not as though the conception of God could not outride such objections; it is rather that such a conception of God reflects little credit on the person who thinks it up. I share, if you like, the well-known outlook of the *bodhisattva*, who forestalls his own beatitude until the last sentient being has attained it; or of Moses and Paul who would rather be stricken from the Book of Life than saved alone. In short, can one live a religious faith to the full without being cut off from others either quantitatively or qualitatively—either from the whole of mankind down the ages or from whatever is human in them and in oneself?

5. UNIVERSALITY AND CONCRETENESS

The problem comes down to this: Can one lead a universal life in the concrete? Is it feasible to live by faith that is at once embodied—incarnational—and transcendent? Is the concrete incompatible with the universal, the categorical with the transcendental?

But here we have only the first part of the problem. The second part emerges when we must contend with people holding different views who claim the right to argue just as we do and to draw conclusions in favor of their own views. After all, the rules must be the same for both sides; I may embrace my neighbor only if I let her embrace me at the same time; I may universalize my belief and reform my religion only if, at the same time, I let my neighbor do the same with hers. Taking this attitude, am I not endangering an entire conception of truth based on the principle of property?

But once our seven-league boots have swept us to the pinnacle of the problem, it is best to start down again along one particular path, to try to shed light on a single facet of the problem and afterwards cite an example to corroborate our words.[2] The aspect I would like to rough out may be focused in the distinction already made between faith and belief.[3]

6. THE ENCOUNTER OF BELIEFS

Let us return to our point of departure and say that I (who for the present purposes can be anybody) live by certain underlying persuasions that express themselves in my personal act of faith: I believe in a God who made the universe, in a Christ who redeemed mankind, in a Spirit who is our pledge of everlasting life, and so forth. For me all these phrases are just translations into a given language understandable in a given tradition, of something that outsoars all utterance. I refer to those dogmas (as they are called) that make sense of my life and convey what truth is for me. I cannot dispense with these phrases because they make up my belief, but neither must I forget that they are phrases, neither more nor less.

On this level I encounter a person who belongs to another religious tradition. She tells me she does not believe in God, she has no idea who Christ is, and she thinks there is no life but the present one we all experience. She may tell me further that she believes in Buddha as an Enlightened One who has pointed out the road to salvation and that salvation consists in blotting out all existence.

The first requisite for dialogue is that we understand each other. The first prerequisite for this understanding on the intellectual level is that we speak the same language, lest we use different words to convey the same idea and therefore take them to mean different things. Now in order to know we speak the same language, we need a lodestar somewhere outside the framework of language: We must be able to point with the finger of the mind, or some other sign, to the 'thing' when we use the same or different words.

Let us assume (which is assuming a great deal, but so we must if we are to make any headway) we have reached agreement about our language and we are using words to signify ideas defined sharply enough to make discussion possible.

The exchange might then take some such form: "I believe in God as embodying the truth that makes sense of my life and the things around me." "I, on the other hand, believe in the nonexistence of such a being and this nonexistence is precisely what enables me to believe in the truth of things and to make sense of my life and the things around me." Here one person makes "God" the keystone of her existence, salvation, and so on, while the other makes her conviction of "no God" the keystone of the same thing. More simply put: The first declares "God is the truth;" the second says, "no-God is the truth."

Both believe in truth, but the phrase "God exists" sums up the truth for one, while for the other the phrase "God does not exist" sums it up. At this point the more exact statement enters: Both have *faith* in the truth, but for the one this faith expresses itself in the *belief* that "God exists," while for the other it expresses itself in the contrary proposition, "God does not exist."

If one said "God exists" and the other, "God does not exist," then *faith* would be the ground of each one's conviction of what her own proposition means, and *belief* would be the conviction set forth in each one's proposition. Even to bluntly refuse any dialogue implies the faith that one possesses the truth and the belief that the formula cannot be sundered from the thing formulated. Affirming absurdity or postulating nothingness can be *beliefs* of the *same faith* that moves others to believe in God or in Humanity.

7. KṚṢṆA AND CHRIST

Here, by acknowledging that a single faith may express itself in contrasting and even contradictory beliefs, dialogue would start. The next step is to understand the other's position, and at once a tremendous difficulty arises. I can never understand her position as she does—and this is the only real understanding between people—unless I share her view; in a word, unless I judge it to be somewhat true. It is contradictory to imagine I understand another's view when at the same time I call it false. I may indeed say I understand my partner in dialogue better than she understands herself. I may say she is mistaken because she contradicts herself, even say I understand her position because I understand her premises;

but clearly I cannot uphold her view as she does unless I share it. When I say I understand a proposition and consider it untrue, in the first place I do not understand it because, by definition, truth alone is intelligible (if I understand a thing I always understand it *sub ratione veritatis);* in the second place I certainly do not understand it in the way of someone who holds it to be true. Accordingly, to understand is to be converted to the truth one understands.[4]

Now the problem becomes even more involved. Let us consider an example: My partner declares that one arrives at salvation through Kṛṣṇa, the supreme epiphany of the Godhead. If I understand *what* he is saying I must simply yield my assent, as he does his, to the truth of that declaration; that is, I share his point of view—even though I may still believe that mine may be subtler and may in fact incorporate his. Otherwise I must say I do not understand *it,* or withdraw intelligibility to an earlier level: I understand *him,* I know what he *means* because I understand that his declaration follows from a series of assumptions that lead him to believe what he says; but I do not share his belief in the truth of those assumptions. Then the problem comes down to understanding these assumptions and their intelligibility. Hence dialogue serves the useful purpose of laying bare our own assumptions and those of others, thereby giving us a more critically grounded conviction of what we hold to be true.

To my mind the most far-reaching conclusions follow from what has been said up to this point, but I have yet a good deal more to say. The real religious or theological task, if you will, begins when the two views meet head-on inside oneself; when dialogue prompts genuine religious pondering, and even a religious crisis, at the bottom of a one's heart; when interpersonal dialogue turns into intrapersonal soliloquy.

Let us suppose I have grasped the basic belief of a vaiṣṇava and therefore share it; in other words I can honestly affirm what an orthodox vaiṣṇava believes. Does this mean I have deserted my original religious position? Are the two beliefs not essentially irreconcilable? Either I believe in Kṛṣṇa or I believe in Christ. Either I am a christian and declare Jesus as the Savior of mankind, or I follow Kṛṣṇa and acknowledge him as the true Savior of humanity. Is it not a double betrayal to try to reconcile these two beliefs, which conflict at every point? Can we find any way out of this dilemma?

At this juncture, the dialogue of which I speak emerges not as a mere academic device or an intellectual amusement, but as a spiritual matter of the first rank, a religious act that itself engages faith, hope, and love. Dialogue is not bare methodology but an essential part of the religious act par excellence: loving God above all things and one's neighbor as oneself. If we believe that our neighbor lies entangled in falsehood and superstition we can hardly love him as ourselves, without a hypocritical, pitying love that moves us to try plucking the mote out of his eye. Love for our neighbor also makes intellectual demands, for as the christian tradition has said over and over again, you cannot love your neighbor as yourself without loving God. Perhaps I can love the other person as *other*, which means as an object to me (as useful, pleasant, kind, beautiful, complementary to me, something of this sort), but I cannot love him as *myself* unless I take my place on the one bit of higher ground that will hold us both—unless I love God. God is the unique locus where my selfhood and my neighbor's coincide, consequently the one place that enables me to love him as he loves his own self without any attempt at molding him.[5]

For this very reason I cannot love God unless I love my neighbor because God is that transcending of my 'I' that puts me in touch with my neighbor. Saint Augustine (could we expect otherwise?) says so word for word: "Because a Man loves his neighbor as himself only if he loves God" *(Diligit enim unusquisque proximum suum tamquam seipsum, si diligit Deum).* Understanding my neighbor means understanding him as he understands himself, which can be done only if I rise above the subject-object dichotomy, cease to know him as an object, and come to know him as myself. Only if there exists a Self in which we communicate does it become possible to know and love another as Oneself. Anyone with half an eye can see what follows and how it upsets the false privacy in which we are inclined to shut ourselves away. True intimacy does not stiffen or deaden us because within that Self (God is not the Other, he is the One) dwell life, dialogue, and love. This is in fact the Trinitarian mystery, but we must not wander from our present topic.

Let no one object that the Gospel commission is not to dialogue with all nations but to go and teach them—in the first place, because here we are not conducting apologetics of any sort and so feel under no obligation to prove the orthodoxy of any view; and in the second place because that commission is cited in a mutilated form and altogether out of context. The complete text makes it quite clear that the 'discipleship' it refers to consists precisely in serving one's fellows and loving them, and they are not served if I am the one who lays down how the master is to be served. Moreover, the commission is purely charismatic—it calls for the power to work miracles. Who would like to throw the first stone?

Be that as it may, no one can fail to see the religious challenge of the situation I have set forth. A really devout mind will ask how we can embrace the faith of our neighbor without going astray in our own. Indeed how can we embrace it at all? Can my faith absorb another's belief? Here I think we have the touchstone for any genuine life of faith in our day: We must believe those who do not believe, just as we must love those who do not love.

8. THE MULTIRELIGIOUS EXPERIENCE

Now I should like to sketch the religious attitude of one embarked on such a venture. She starts by making a real, heartfelt, unselfish effort—a bold and hazardous one—to understand the belief, the world, the archetypes, the culture, the mythical and conceptual background, the emotional and historical associations of her friends from the inside. In short, she seriously attempts an existential incarnation of herself into another world—which obviously involves prayer, initiation, study, and worship. She does this not by way of trial but rather with a spirit of faith in a truth that transcends us and a goodness that upholds us when we truly love our neighbor—which does not mean, as I have said, eliminating the intellect from this enterprise. It is not experimentation but a genuine experience undergone within one's own faith. Consequently that experience is forbidden, or rather does not become possible, unless she has established in herself the distinction between her faith (ever transcendent, unutterable, and open) and her belief (an intellectual, emotional, and cultural embodiment of that faith within the framework of a particular tradition that, yes, demands her loyalty, but not that she betray the rest of humankind). I need hardly add that not everyone is called to such an undertaking, nor is everyone capable of it. Besides a particular cast of mind, it presupposes perhaps a special constellation in one's character and background that enables one to undergo the experience without any taint of exoticism, exhibitionism, or simply unremitting intellectualism. In a word, we need a kind of connaturality to go through that venture in a genuine way. I repeat: It does not mean experimenting either with one's own faith or with that of others. Faith can only be lived, but living it may at times demand risking it in order to remain faithful.

Moreover, this risk of faith must be understood as emerging from one's own faith itself; not from doubting what one believes, but deepening and enriching it. This risk should not be understood as an intellectual or religious curiosity but as a dynamic of faith itself, which discloses another religious world in one's neighbor that we can neither ignore nor brush aside, but must try to take up, integrate into our own. What is more, when faith claims universality, the faith of the neighbor automatically becomes a problem that cannot be evaded.

Abstract principles do not enable one to foresee what will happen in such an encounter; she must be prepared to stake everything she is and believes, not because she harbors doubts about it, nor yet because she says at the back of her mind that she is conducting some sort of methodological *epoché* (which at this juncture in history would be unnatural and unthinkable[6]), but because the venture hazards—or to be more precise, let us say makes possible—a conversion so thoroughgoing that the convictions and beliefs she had hitherto held may vanish or undergo a far-reaching change. Unquestionably the venture is perilous; you gamble your life. Hardly anyone would be equal to it but for the very drive of faith that invites us to hazard our life without fear, even to lose it.

9. INTERPRETING THE EXPERIENCE

Only afterward can we describe what happens. I shall attempt to do this in the space of a few paragraphs.

We can live only by truth; falsehood offers the mind no nourishment.[7] If my partner believes in Kṛṣṇa it is because he believes Kṛṣṇa embodies truth, and this belief enters into the very truth of what he believes. I can understand this only if I also believe in the truth he believes, perhaps under rather a different guise. Whatever can be said of objective truth, religious belief is a highly personal and so subjective thing; the faith that saves is always personal and subjective. The Kṛṣṇa of our dialogue is not a historical or mythological figure but the Kṛṣṇa of faith, of my interlocutor's personal faith. His belief is the one I must assume, sharing his truth, the truth of the Kṛṣṇa of faith.

My own faith must be strong enough for me to do this—open and deep enough to work its way into the vaiṣṇava world and share that world's ups and downs. First of all, my faith must be naked enough to be clothed in all those forms with no misgivings about slipping into heresy or apostasy. (Anyone who *thinks* he will be betraying his faith should not and cannot embark on this venture.) Then, in a second moment, my intrareligious soliloquy will have to blend my earlier beliefs with those acquired later, according to my lights and conscience (this entire procedure, of course, is also valid for my partner).

My partner in dialogue will then judge whether what I have learned

of Kṛṣṇa is sound or not. I will have to give him an account of my belief
and he will tell me whether what I say about Kṛṣṇa—one of the epiphanies of God and his love for humanity, eminently one of God's names, a
real symbol of the freedom of God, and so forth—represents fundamental
belief in Kṛṣṇa or not.

Once this first step has been taken, I must next explain to myself and
also to my interlocutor how I blend this new religious experience of mine
with belief in Christ.

Here an alternative lies before me: Either I have ceased to be a christian—belief in Kṛṣṇa has supplanted my belief in Christ; I have found a
loftier, fuller divine reality in Kṛṣṇa than in Christ—or else I am able to
establish a special kind of bond between the two that both religions, or at
least one of them, *can* acknowledge and accept (I do not say they already
have accepted it).

If the specific problem is talked over not only with the uninvolve-
ment befitting investigators into religion but also on a spiritual level high
enough to rule out what may be called fundamentalist microdoxy, then
we could in most cases reach a solution where each tradition finds the
other's reading of it valid, therefore at least partially orthodox. I say "partially" because each belief is integrated into a wider whole, which does
not need to be accepted by the other party.

This example brings in a set of propositions that may answer the
requirements of orthodoxy on both sides. With regard to traditional Christianity I would say: The unutterable, transcendent, everlasting God has
never left us without witness to the divine reality, and God has always
wisely looked after God's creatures. That one mystery at work since the
dawn of time, whose delight is to be with the children of "Men," has dis-
closed to them God's kindness, the godliness of love, the gladness of living, the nature of worship, and a set of rites with which to give their
earthly existence meaning. That same mystery, hidden away for aeons,
unveils itself in Christ in the last days with a special historical consciousness so that the incorporation of the peoples into the *historical* dynamism
of the world entails a certain relationship with Christ.

What may trouble the christian mind about this sketch is the nature of
the relationship between Christ and Kṛṣṇa. I shall make no attempt to deal
with this problem at present. It is enough to say, first, that the difficulty
strikes me as greco-western, or rather philosophical, more than strictly
christian; second, that the identity need not be one of personal substance—
a functional identity will do. I am not evading the problem; I merely point
out its parameters. Perhaps mythic terms best serve to intimate the

connection between Christ and Kṛṣṇa, but obviously the connection is something other than flat identity. I mean there is no need to say Christ is Kṛṣṇa, or the one a foreshadowing or fulfillment of the other in order to indicate their special relationship. At this point we feel the lack of a theology dealing with the encounter between religions. The problem of the one and the many also crops up here, albeit in a new form. But the place of vaiṣṇavism in the christian economy of salvation might very well be found here, within the framework of a universal economy of salvation and in a certain mysterious presence of the Lord in a multitude of epiphanies.

Something parallel could be said from the vaiṣṇava side. We do not propose to argue whether the theology of Kṛṣṇa is the most perfect there is, blending the human element in its fullness with the godly one within the strictest demands of the Absolute. What may trouble the vaiṣṇava mind is the peculiar emphasis laid upon historicity, perhaps to the detriment of an ever-original and genuine religious experience that does not need to rely on the faith of others but discovers by itself the living symbol of belief. What may further bother a devotee of Kṛṣṇa is what he feels to be the christian reductionism of religion to morals and of Christ to a single man. Perhaps christians could answer and the dialogue could go on, but we merely wish to show that belief in Kṛṣṇa need not rule out acknowledging Jesus as an epiphany of God at one particular moment in history.

The basic issue for discussion would be the ultimate nature of the two divine epiphanies. While the christian will say that Christ is the fullness and apex of God's every *epiphany*, the vaiṣṇava will be moved to say that nothing can outdo the *theophany* of Kṛṣṇa. Nevertheless the difficulty can be overcome by mutual understanding. In terms of belonging to one or the other religious body (according to traditional standard, although nothing can halt the growth of tradition), the difficulty is for the time being insuperable, but we are now talking about something else, about dialogue that *is* true dialogue and therefore brings each side to understand and share the basic attitude of the other. Here the difficulty is not insuperable because, in the first place, when the matter is raised in this down-to-earth, existential way, one may perfectly well say that the heart of the matter is not deciding who holds the 'objective' primacy because by living in accordance with their particular persuasions and beliefs both will attain to what they sincerely believe; in the second place, because the question of Christ and Kṛṣṇa is not a speculation outside time and so defies answer by a timeless and abstract reason alone. Only historical eschatology can adequately tell us whether Christ fulfills Kṛṣṇa, or Kṛṣṇa,

Christ, or none supersedes the other. The question *as such* is childish, as
though I were to argue that my daddy writes better poetry than your
daddy (forgetting that each poem is unique for each child and there can
be no comparing of poems qua poems). *In you* and *in me* the question is
premature (neither of us need be argued out of his belief); *in* us—that is,
insofar as it helps us toward mutual understanding and the ultimate goal
of all mankind—history (personal and collective) will have the last word.
Meanwhile a wholesome emulation will harm neither side. Things might
go farther; the vaiṣṇava may perhaps admit the also historical nature of
Kṛṣṇa, thereby opening the door for the christian to acknowledge the
growth—hence the metamorphosis—Christ "undergoes" down the ages.
The christian may perhaps admit the also transhistorical nature of Christ,
thereby opening the door for the vaiṣṇava to acknowledge the mystery—
hence the pluriformity—Kṛṣṇa "undergoes" down the ages. But this is
only a beginning because the continuation of the dialogue has to produce
its own rules and categories.

10. FAITH AND BELIEFS

I need hardly say that neither every vaiṣṇava nor every christian is automatically prepared, in intellect and spirit, to come thus face to face—at
bottom because very few have had the experience and so it has not been
worked out theologically. Here history might teach a mighty lesson by
reminding us how jewish, greek, zoroastrian, and other 'dogmas' seeped
into the christian mind, making themselves part of what we nowadays
call the common christian heritage. The same would apply for a theology
of Kṛṣṇa—in both cases.

For the moment let us content ourselves with some philosophical and
theological considerations centering on the distinction we have drawn
between faith and belief. For the sake of simplicity I shall start from christian assumptions that commend themselves as a succinct and intelligible
frame of reference to the western mind, but that can be readily transposed
into those of other religious traditions. Let me add at once that in so doing
I jump to no conclusions as to whether the christian approach can be uni-
versalized in a way others cannot. At the present time I do not wish to
grapple with that problem.

The main function of faith is to connect me with transcendence, with
what stands above me, with what I am not (yet). Faith is the connection
with the beyond, however you choose to envision it. So one thing faith

effects is salvation: The business of faith is preeminently to save us. Now for this, faith cannot be couched in universal forms that express it fully. If this were possible, faith would become so earthbound that it would no longer provide a bridge "binding" us (Latin *religare*) to something loftier than ourselves. Faith may lend itself more or less to ideation, but no set of words, no expression, can ever exhaust it. Yet it needs to be embodied in ideas and formulas—so much so that faith incapable of expressing itself at all would not be human faith. Such expressions we have called beliefs, in accordance with what tradition has always felt.

Were things otherwise, my faith would cut me off from others rather than unite me with them, faith would estrange us from each other instead of binding us together, and religion would express horizontal divergences instead of vertical convergence. That history, for countless reasons, bears witness to both trends in the actual evolution of religions does not invalidate what I am saying; it only shows that faith has been confused with belief. The moment dialogue ceases and we live isolated from one another, faith inevitably becomes identified with belief and fosters exclusivism with all the results that history in general and the history of religions in particular have made so painfully familiar.

Yet our distinction presents special features. Faith cannot be equated with belief, but faith always needs a belief to be faith. Belief is not faith, but it must convey faith. A disembodied faith is not faith. A belief that does not always point to a beyond that outsoars and in a sense annihilates it is not belief but fanaticism. Faith finds expression in belief, and through it people normally arrive at faith. Where people live in a homogeneous cultural world, most never notice the tension between faith and belief. They look on dogmas, which are simply authoritative formulations of belief, almost as if they were faith itself, half forgetting that they are dogmas *of* faith. When cultural change or an encounter between religions robs the notions hitherto bound up with faith of their solidity and unmistakable correspondence to faith, naturally a crisis erupts. But this is a crisis of belief, not faith. Undoubtedly the bond between the two is intimate; it is in fact constitutive because thought itself requires language, and belief is the language of faith. Hence what begins as a crisis of belief turns into a crisis of faith, as a rule due to the intransigence of those who will tolerate no change because they do not distinguish between faith and belief.

When a christian says she believes in God the Father, in Christ, and in the Holy Spirit, she does not believe in a *deus ex machina ad usum christianorum,* but a reality of truth subsisting everywhere, even outside the bounds of her own experience. But she conveys this truth in language inherited from her own tradition, and she can grasp its meaning only in those terms. When she comes into contact with a different form of religious expression, her first impulse will be to suppose her interlocutor is talking about some reality apart from and essentially different from her own: She will think of false 'Gods', false religion, and so on. After a deeper look, she will perceive that at bottom they mean a similar thing, although the other refers to it with concepts she may judge inadequate or erroneous. Thus one of the primary tasks facing theology is the tremendous one of finding parallels and features in other religions that complement each other, as well as points of conflict. But no one can deny that the ultimate purpose of the two religions is the same. Unless the spadework, entailing all we have indicated, is done at the outset, and a good deal more besides, misunderstandings will almost inevitably accumulate, even today, to bedevil nine-tenths of the relations among religions and therefore among people.

At times the obvious will have to be explained, but patience seems to be an intellectual as well as a moral virtue. Doesn't faith itself call on us to break out of our limitations and constantly die to ourselves to rise again in newness of life? I mean that the christian's connatural attitude toward the faith of others seems to embrace, absorb, and embody rather than repulse, expel, and shut out. Possibly these are two anthropological bents marking different cultural situations, but in any event the disposition to attract rather than repel strikes me as more consonant with the christian dynamism.

I shall not attempt now to develop an entire doctrine of the Mystery—whom christians recognize in Christ and other religions in other symbols—present and at work in every religion, usually in a dark and enigmatic way. I will only try to set forth the spiritual attitude that impels me to seek to integrate, as far as possible, the religiousness of others into my own before asserting mine in order to compare and judge. Let us only dip into the experience of trying to understand a form of religion from inside, and we will perceive the authenticity and truth with which it is charged, whatever the weakness and even immorality its outward features exhibit (as in certain forms of devotion to Kṛṣṇa or certain interpretations of christianity). What I should like to stress is the way faith prompts one to link up different kinds of religion. We may not see eye-to-eye about how to do this, but theology today must work out the means if it is to survive and stop being archaeology.

The solution is not so easy, not only due to historical and cultural estrangements, but also because the relation between faith and belief is not so simple that we might consider belief the mere costume of faith and so infer that it is all a matter of taste for one vestment or another. Belief, the garb or expression of faith, is part and parcel of faith itself inasmuch as our self-understanding belongs to the very nature of that being whose nature is precisely understanding—even if it is not exclusively understanding. I cannot strip off my belief— insofar as it is a real belief, that is, insofar as I believe in 'it' (or more simply said, I believe)—without touching and even transforming my faith.

In a word, I am not simplistically saying that all beliefs are merely expressions of one and the same faith because faith without belief does not exist—not for those who believe. We are not *logos* alone, but the *logos* is something more than the mere instrument of us. This is why to speak of the transcendent unity of religions is true as long as it does not remain the immanent 'truth' of the different religious traditions under discussion.[8] The *relativity* of beliefs does not mean their *relativism.* Our human task is to establish a religious dialogue that, although it transcends the logos— and belief—does not neglect or ignore them.

I am only trying to say that faith must not be confused with belief. Many a misunderstanding has risen from confusing them, or rather from not adequately distinguishing between them.

The experience of faith is a primal anthropological act that every person performs in one way or another, rather like the way we begin to use reason upon its awakening, although no one can foresee along what lines our minds will work or what our first thoughts will be. The act of faith itself has saving power. Theologians will hasten to say (and we need not contradict them) that the act of faith can be made by a human being only when God's grace prompts it. In any event the act of faith is not only transcendent, uniting us with what surpasses us, but also transcendental. It exceeds all possible formulations, and it makes them possible because it also precedes them. Faith is a constitutive human dimension.[9]

At any rate the experience of faith is a human experience that will not be contained in any formula but in fact couches itself in what I have called formulas of belief. Each of us perforce gives utterance to the deepest of our impressions, but to this end we must use language that binds it up with a given human tradition, we lay hold of images and symbols that belong to a cultural group. We will make our faith known in a set of beliefs that we will perhaps call dogmas, expressing in intellectual terms what we wish to convey. Obviously these terms may be multifarious; in fact they are necessarily multivalent.

I am not suggesting that all beliefs are equal and interchangeable; I am saying that in a certain respect they exhibit the same nature, which makes dialogue, and even dialectics, possible. Moreover, I assert they are generally equivalent in that every belief has a similar function: to express our faith, that faith which is the anthropological dimension through which we reach our goal—in christian language, our salvation.

Clearly there remains the major difficulty of ascertaining how deep each belief delves into faith or how satisfactorily it expresses faith. Certain creedal formulas deriving from a naive, underdeveloped cast of mind may not answer the needs of more highly developed people. This truth emerges at every turn in the history of religions, in the encounter and cross-fertilization between differing religious traditions, in the dialogue and sometimes the skirmishes between different schools of thought within the same tradition. We have an example of it in much of what goes on in the cultural and religious world of the catholicism people call 'roman': The noble monolithic solidity of that world breaks down into various parts, into all the colors of the rainbow, through a thoroughgoing change of beliefs within a single experience of faith.

The problem we are considering reaches far beyond these limits and lights on the farthest human horizon where the issue of religious encounter presents itself. For obvious reasons we can only rough out the problem here. One way or another we are all embarked on the venture. Dead calm is as fraught with danger as a roaring gale. While we are on the high seas, we must have oars and sails.

NOTES

1. No need to remind the reader that *parish*, Latin *paroecia*, comes from the Greek πάροικος, from παρά and οἶκος, to sojourn, dwell beside, be beside the house, a neighbor, but also a stranger. Cf. πάροχος, a public purveyor.

2. Cf. R. Panikkar, *Myth, Faith and Hermeneutics* (New York: Paulist Press, 1978), chapter 14 on *karma*, which expands this example.

3. Cf. *ibid.*, chapter 6.

4. Cf. R. Panikkar, "Verstehen als Ueberzeugstein," in *Neue Anthropologie*, vol. 7, edited by H.G. Gadamer and P. Vogler (Stuttgart: Thieme, 1975), pp. 132–67.

5. Cf. *Myth, Faith and Hermeneutics*, op. cit., chapter 9.

6. Cf. chapter 5: "Epochê in the religious encounter."

7. Cf. the two following quotations, the first of Thomas Aquinas citing St. Ambrose (Glossa Lombardi, P.L 191, 1651): "Omne verum, a quocumque dicatur, a Spiritu Sancto est." *Summa Theologiae* I-II. q. 109, a. 1, ad 1. And the second from Meister Eckhart: "Falsum vero, a quocumque dicatur, nulli dicitur." In Iohan. I, 51 (Nr. 277 of the *Opera omnia*). Cf. also *Sermo* XX (Nr. 198).

8. Cf. F. Schuon, *De l'unité transcendante des religions* (Paris: Gallimard, 1948) of which there is an English translation (London: Faber and Faber, 1953) and which has recently been resurrected in the North American scene (cf. *Journal of the American Academy of Religion* 44, 4, December 1976), pp. 715–24.

9. Cf. *Myth, Faith and Hermeneutics*, op. cit., chapter 6.

4

The Rules of the Game in the Religious Encounter

śāstra-yonitvāt
Learned traditions being the
source (of knowledge).
—BS I, 1, 3*

T HE MEETING OF RELIGIONS IS AN INESCAPABLE FACT TODAY. I would like to formulate one principle that should govern the meeting of religions and draw from it a few corollary consequences.

The principle is this: *The Religious encounter must be a truly religious one.* Anything short of this simply will not do.

Some consequences are the following:

*Brahman is the *yoni* of the *śāstrat,* says Śaṅkara in his commentary. The Great Scriptures, the human traditions, are the womb of knowledge and *brahman* also the source not in a vicious, but in a vital circle.

1. IT MUST BE FREE
FROM PARTICULAR APOLOGETICS

If the christian or buddhist or believer in whatever religion approaches another religious person with the a priori idea of defending his own religion by all (obviously honest) means, we shall have perhaps a valuable defense of that religion and undoubtedly exciting discussions, but no religious dialogue, no encounter, much less a mutual enrichment and fecundation. One need not give up one's beliefs and convictions—surely not, but we must eliminate any apologetics if we really want to meet a person from another religious tradition. By apologetics I understand that part of the science of a particular religion that tends to prove the truth and value of that religion. Apologetics has its function and its proper place, but not here in the meeting of religions.

2. IT MUST BE FREE
FROM GENERAL APOLOGETICS

I understand very well the anguish of the modern religious person seeing the wave of 'unreligion' and even 'irreligion' in our times, and yet I would consider it misguided to fall prey to such a fear by founding a kind of religious league—not to say crusade—of the 'pious', of religious people of all confessions, defenders of the 'sacred rights' of religion.

If to forget the first corollary would indicate a lack of confidence in our partner and imply that he is wrong and that I must 'convert' him, to neglect this second point would betray a lack of confidence in the truth of religion itself and represent an indiscriminate accusation against 'modern' Man. The attitude proposing a common front for religion or against unbelief may be understandable, but it is not a religious attitude—not according to the present degree of religious consciousness.

3. ONE MUST FACE
THE CHALLENGE OF CONVERSION

If the encounter is to be an authentically religious one, it must be totally loyal to truth and open to reality. The genuinely religious spirit is not loyal only to the past; it also keeps faith with the present. A religious person is neither a fanatic nor someone who already has all the answers. She is also a seeker, a pilgrim making her own uncharted way; the track ahead is yet virgin, inviolate. She finds each moment new and is but the more pleased to see in this both the beauty of a personal discovery and the depth of a perennial treasure that the ancestors in the faith have handed down.

Yet, to enter the new field of the religious encounter is a challenge and a risk. The religious person enters this arena without prejudices and pre-conceived solutions, knowing full well that she may in fact have to lose a particular belief or particular religion altogether. She trusts in truth. She enters unarmed and ready to be converted herself. She may lose her life— she may also be born again.

4. THE HISTORICAL DIMENSION IS NECESSARY BUT NOT SUFFICIENT

Religion is not just *Privatsache,* nor just a vertical 'link' with the Absolute, but it is also a connection with humanity; it has a tradition, a historical dimension. The religious encounter is not merely the meeting of two or more people in their capacity as strictly private individuals, severed from their respective religious traditions. A truly religious person bears at once the burden of tradition and the riches of her ancestors. But she is not an official representative, as it were, speaking only on behalf of others or from sheer hearsay: She is a living member of a community, a believer in a living religious tradition.

The religious encounter must deal with the historical dimension, not stop with it. It is not an encounter of historians, still less of archaeologists, but it is a living dialogue, a place for creative thinking and imaginative new ways that do not break with the past but continue and extend it.

This is hardly to disparage historical considerations; quite the contrary, I would insist on an understanding of the traditions in question that is at once deep and broad. The first implies not only that we be familiar with the age-old tradition, but also with the present state of that particular religion. Taking as our example that bundle of religions that goes under the name of 'Hinduism', I would contend that a profound understanding of this tradition cannot ignore its evolution up to the present day, unless we are ready to accept an arbitrary and skewed interpretation. A scholar may indeed limit herself to Vedic studies, for example, but someone engaged in a truly religious encounter can scarcely justify basing her understanding of hinduism solely on Sāyana's interpretation of the Vedas while completely ignoring that of, say, Dayānanda or Aurobindo (the relative merits of various interpretations is not our concern here). Similarly no modern christian can be satisfied with Jerome's interpretation of the Bible or with the medieval understanding of it.

Our point is that no study of an idea, cultural pattern, or religious tradition is adequate unless we consider all its possibilities, just as no botanist can claim to know a seed until he knows the plant that grows up from that seed. Moreover, in this case, the movement of understanding is dynamic and reciprocal. Thus I would contend not only that any study of the nature of *dharma,* for instance, is incomplete if it does not consider the present-day understanding of that concept, but also that the ancient notion is likely to be only partially understood if its development up to modern times is left aside. This also implies that someone who tries to understand the notion of *dharma,* whether in ancient or modern India, cannot do so *in vacuo:* The very words he uses are already culturally charged with meanings and values.

Further, the traditions must also be understood in a broader perspective, one that oversteps the provincial boundaries of geography and culture. To understand the hindu tradition—staying with our example—we cannot limit ourselves to the indian subcontinent: The impact of buddhism on eastern and central Asia is so well known that I need only mention it; the Rāmāyaṇa and the Mahābhārata have been shaping forces in many countries south of Burma; Śiva is worshiped in Indonesia. Pursuing these avenues of research is not a mere academic tangent but serves to complete the picture we begin to see through indigenous sources. Even more, we cannot limit our attention to past cross-cultural contacts and ignore the multitude of contemporary instances. Many an indic value asserts itself today on the shores of California and in universities throughout Europe. Whether the change in climate distorts or enhances the original values is a separate question; the influence is unmistakable. In return, Western values have, for better or for worse, deeply penetrated not only the great cities but also the most remote villages of India. Given such developments, can our understanding of indic religions remain imprisoned in a scholarly ivory tower whose drawbridge was raised when the muslims arrived? The phenomenon of feedback does not refer only to the diffusion of gadgets and other technological paraphernalia throughout the world; popularized ideas from every continent now travel literally at the speed of light to the farthest corners of the planet and the deepest recesses of the human psyche.

The importance of the historical dimension notwithstanding, what is at stake in the religious encounter is not 'History of Religions' or even

'Comparative Religion', but a living and demanding faith. Faith is life and life cannot be reduced to imitating the past or merely reinterpreting it. The religious encounter is a religious event.

5. IT IS NOT JUST
A CONGRESS OF PHILOSOPHY

Needless to say, without a certain degree of philosophy no encounter is possible, and yet the religious dialogue is not just a meeting of philosophers to discuss intellectual problems. Religions are much more than doctrines. Within one religion there may even be a pluralism of doctrines. To pin down a religion to a certain definite doctrinal set is to kill that religion. No particular doctrine *as such* can be considered the unique and irreplaceable expression of a religion. Indeed, *denying* a particular doctrine without overcoming it or substituting another for it may be heresy, but no religion is satisfied to be *only* orthodoxy, ignoring orthopraxis. To be sure, creation, God, *nirvāṇa*, and the like are important concepts, but the real religious issue lies elsewhere: in the real 'thing' meant by these and other notions. I may share with my muslim colleague the same idea of the transcendence of God, and he may be of the same opinion as his buddhist partner regarding the law of *karma,* and yet none of us may feel compelled to change our religion.

Clearly, I need to understand what the other is saying, that is, what the other means to say, and this involves a new understanding of interpretation itself. Now the golden rule of any hermeneutic is that the interpreted thing can recognize itself in the interpretation. In other words, any interpretation from outside a tradition has to coincide, at least phenomenologically, with an interpretation from within, that is, with the believer's viewpoint. To label a *mūrtipūjaka,* an idol-worshiper, for instance, using idol as it is commonly understood in the judeo-christian-muslim context rather than beginning with what the worshiper affirms of himself, is to transgress this rule. An entire philosophical and religious context underpins the notion of *mūrti;* we cannot simply impose alien categories on it. Although the problem remains formidable, one of the most positive achievements of our times is that we have come to realize that there are no immutable categories that can serve as absolute criteria for judging everything under the sun.

Briefly then, I would like to consider two principles that govern any sound hermeneutical method and the way in which they may be critically coordinated.

The *principle of homogeneity.* An ancient conviction, held in both East and West, has it that only like can know like. In other words, a concept can be properly understood and evaluated only from within a homogeneous context. Every cultural value has a definite sphere where it is valid and meaningful; any unwarranted extrapolation can only lead to confusion and misunderstanding. Nothing is more harmful than hurried syntheses or superficial parallelisms. Here is the place and the great value of tradi-tional theology, which provides the internal understanding of a religion, the self-understanding of that religion as it is lived. Without this previous work, fruitful interreligious encounters would not be possible.

The *dialogical principle.* Applying the principle of homogeneity with strict rigor or exclusivity would paralyze a critical approach and halt any progress toward mutual understanding. I may understand the world-view that underlies the religious practice of another—human sacrifice, for instance—yet I may still consider it immature, wrong, even barbaric. Why is this? It may be that I have developed another form of awareness or dis-covered another principle of understanding that leads me to see the inad-equacy of a certain notion (here that which upholds human sacrifice). I may have acquired a perspective under which I am able to criticize another point of view; perhaps I can now detect incongruencies or assumptions that are no longer tenable. In this sort of activity, the dialog-ical principle is at work. Only through an internal or external dialogue can we become aware of uncritical or unwarranted assumptions. This dia-logue does not merely look for new sources of information, but leads to a deeper understanding of the other and of oneself. We are all learning to welcome light and criticism, even when it comes from foreign shores.

Coordination: By themselves, each of these principles is barren and unsatisfying; together they provide a means of cross-cultural understand-ing that is both valid and critical. Those concerned with indian traditions, whatever their background, are convinced that they cannot disregard the methodological principles of modern critical scholarship. At the same time, they are quite aware that neither science nor western categories con-stitute an absolute standard, nor do they have universal applicability. These two insights give rise to the coordination of the two principles. Here we cannot elaborate the guidelines for such a coordination. It is enough to say that the effort must be truly interdisciplinary and interpersonal, involving not only the traditional fields of 'academia', but also the people whose religions we are considering. No statement is valid and meaning-ful if it cannot be heard, understood, and, in a way, verified by all those concerned and not merely bandied about by the literati.

Indeed, philosophical clarification is today extremely important because by and large religions have lived in restricted areas and closed circles and have tended to identify a particular set of philosophical doctrines—because they were useful to convey the religious message—with the core of the religion. The mutual enrichment of real encounter and the consequent liberation may be enormous.

6. IT IS NOT ONLY
A THEOLOGICAL SYMPOSIUM

As an authentic venture, the true religious encounter is filled with a sort of prophetic charisma; it is not just an effort to make the outsider understand my point. Indeed, at least according to more than one school, true theology also claims to be a charismatic deepening in meaning of a particular revelation or religion. Generally, however, theologians are more concerned with explaining given data than with exploring tasks ahead. Obviously hermeneutics is indispensable; but still more important is to *grasp* what is to be interpreted prior to any (more or less plausible) explanation. Theology may furnish the tools for mutual understanding but must remember that the religious encounter imperative today is a new problem and that the tools furnished by the theologies are not fit to master the new task unless purified, chiseled, and perhaps forged anew in the very encounter.

As an example of what is needed, we may use the notion of homeomorphism, which does not connote a mere comparison of concepts from one tradition with those of another. I want to suggest this notion as the correlation between points of two different systems so that a point in one system corresponds to a point in the other. The method does not imply that one system is better (logically, morally, or whatever) than the other nor that the two points are interchangeable: You cannot, as it were, transplant a point from one system to the other. The method only discovers homeomorphous correlations.

Now homeomorphism, as we have already said, is not identical with analogy, although they are related. Homeomorphism does not mean that two notions are analogous, that is, partially the same and partially different, because this implies that both share in a 'tertiam quid' that provides the basis for the analogy. Homeomorphism means rather that the notions play equivalent roles, that they occupy homologous places within their respective systems. Homeomorphism is perhaps a kind of existential-functional analogy.

An example may clarify what I mean.

It is quite clearly false, for instance, to equate the upaniṣadic concept of *Brahman* with the biblical notion of *Yahweh*. Nevertheless it is equally unsatisfactory to say that these concepts have nothing whatever in common. True, their context and contents are utterly different; they are not mutually translatable, nor do they have a direct relationship. But they are homologous; each plays a similar role, albeit in different cultural settings. They both refer to a highest value and an absolute term. On the other hand, we cannot say that *Brahman* is provident and even transcendent or that *Yahweh* is all-pervading, without attributes, and so forth. Nevertheless we can assert that both function homologously within their own cultures.

To give another example, an examination of the traditional indian notion of *karma* and the modern western understanding of historicity under the aegis of this principle could reveal a common homologous role: Each one stands for that temporal ingredient of the human being that transcends individuality.[1] Even more intriguing, perhaps, would be a consideration that homologizes the indian notion of Īśvara (Lord) and the western idea of Christ.[2]

Whatever shape it will take, whatever contents it will carry, I am convinced that a new theology (though this very name means nothing to a buddhist) will emerge precisely out of these encounters between sincere and enlightened believers of the various religious traditions.

Yet the religious encounter is not a mere theological reflection. Theologies—in the widest sense of the word— have a given basis: They are efforts at intelligibility of a given religious tradition and generally within that tradition itself *(fides quaerens intellectum)*. But here we do not have such a belief or such a basis. There is neither a common given nor an accepted basis, revelation, event, or even tradition. Both the very subject matter and the method are to be determined in the encounter itself. There is no common language at the outset. Short of this radical understanding, the encounter of religions becomes a mere cultural entertainment.

7. IT IS NOT MERELY
AN ECCLESIASTICAL ENDEAVOR

To be sure, the dialogue among religions may take place at different levels, and on each level it has its peculiarities. Official encounter among representatives of the world's organized religious groups is today an inescapable duty. Yet the issues in such meetings are not the same as those in a dialogue that tries to reach the deepest possible level. Ecclesiastical dignitaries are bound to preserve tradition; they must consider the multitude of believers who follow that religion, for and to whom they are responsible. They are faced with practical and immediate problems; they must discover ways to tolerate, to collaborate, to understand. But in general they cannot risk new solutions. They have to approve and put into practice already proven fruitful ways. But where are those proofs to come from? The religious encounter we have in mind will certainly pave the way for ecclesiastical meetings and vice versa but must be differentiated and separated from them.

8. IT IS A RELIGIOUS ENCOUNTER IN FAITH, HOPE, AND LOVE

The word *religious* here does not stand for mere piety or commitment. It stands for the integrality of the total person engaged in the dialogue. In other words, it does not stand for 'religious' ideas or ideals exclusively, as if the encounter may only deal with doctrinal issues of common interest. We are also discussing *ourselves* and putting the whole of us at the negotiation table, as already suggested in the third rule.

This means that a truly religious encounter is never totally objectifiable. We do not put objectified 'beliefs' on discussion, but believers, we, ourselves. This is why the mere logical principle of noncontradiction is not enough (necessary as it is) to govern the entire meeting. I may believe that the doctrine x is the highest possible way to express one particular truth, or just the Mystery, so to speak. You may believe that it is the doctrine y that fulfills the requirement, both being different. There is no possible compromise. There would be contradiction if some of us were to believe that within an agreed context x and y could be the case, but there is no contradiction in the fact that you believe y *and* I x. A believing x and B believing y are only contrary situations that can still communicate and struggle further.

I may put it with christian vocabulary, apologizing for this, and yet I think it has a more universal meaning.

By *faith* I mean an attitude that transcends the simple data and the dogmatic formulations of the different confessions as well; that attitude that reaches an understanding even when words and concepts differ because it pierces them, as it were, goes deep down to that realm that is the religious realm par excellence. We do not discuss systems but realities and the way in which these realities manifest themselves so that they also make sense for our partner.

By *hope* I understand that attitude which, hoping against all hope, is able to leap over not only the initial human obstacles, our weakness and unconscious adherences, but also over all kinds of purely profane views and into the heart of the dialogue, as if urged from above to perform a sacred duty.

By *love*, finally, I mean that impulse, that force impelling us to our fellow-beings and leading us to discover in them what is lacking in us. To be sure, real love does not aim for victory in the encounter. It longs for common recognition of the truth, without blotting out the differences or muting the various melodies in the single polyphonic symphony.

9. SOME PRACTICAL LESSONS

What do these rules mean in practice? The chief lessons gleaned from my experience could be summarized as follows:

There must be *equal preparation* for the encounter on both sides, and this means cultural as well as theological preparation. Any dialogue— including the religious one—depends on the cultural settings of the part- ners. To overlook the cultural differences that give rise to different religious beliefs is to court unavoidable misunderstandings. The first function of the dialogue is to discover the ground where the dialogue may properly take place.

There must be real *mutual trust* between those involved in the encounter, something that is possible only when all the cards are on the table, that is, when neither partner 'brackets' his personal beliefs.[3]

The *different issues* (theological, practical, institutional, etc.) have to be carefully distinguished; otherwise there is going to be confusion.

A Christian Example

Christ is the Lord, but the Lord is neither only Jesus nor does my under- standing exhaust the meaning of the word.

Church, as the sociological dimension of religion, is the organism of salvation (by definition), but the Church is not coextensive with the visible christian church.

Christendom is the socioreligious structure of christianity and as such is a religion like any other. It must be judged on its own merits without any special privileges.

God wills that all Men should reach salvation. Here salvation is that which is considered to be the end, goal, destination, or destiny of Man, however this may be conceived.

There is no salvation without faith, but this is not the privilege of christians nor of any special group.

The means of salvation are to be found in any authentic religion (old or new) because a Man follows a particular religion because in it he believes he finds the ultimate fulfillment of his life.

Christ is the only mediator, but he is not the monopoly of christians and, in fact, he is present and effective in any authentic religion, whatever the form or the name. Christ is the symbol, which christians call by this name, of the ever-transcending but equally ever-humanly immanent Mystery. Now these principles should be confronted with parallel humanist, buddhist, and other principles, and then one should be able to detect points of convergence and of discrepancy with all the required qualifications. Further, the christian principles have no a priori paradigmatic value, so it is not a question of just searching for possible equivalents elsewhere. The fair procedure is to start from all possible starting points and witness to the actual encounters taking place along the way.

Summing up

The religious encounter is a religious and hence sacred act through which we are taken up by the truth and by loyalty to the 'three worlds' with no further aim or intention. In this creative religious act the very vitality of religion manifests itself.

NOTES

1. Cf. R. Panikkar, *Hermeneutics,* op. cit., chapter 14.
2. Cf. R. Panikkar, *The Unknown Christ of Hinduism* (Maryknoll, N.Y.: Orbis, Revised & enlarged edition 1981), pp. 148–62.
3. See chapter 5.

5

Epochê in the Religious Encounter

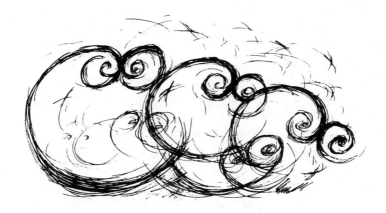

Nothing is more outwardly visible than
the secrets of the heart,
nothing more obvious than what one
attempts to conceal.
—*Chung Yung* I, 1, 3*

1. PROLOGUE

INTERRELIGIOUS DIALOGUE IS TODAY UNAVOIDABLE; IT IS A religious imperative and a historical duty for which we must suitably prepare. But we often hear more talk about interreligious dialogue than actual dialogue. In order to sidestep this pitfall, I would like to begin again by stressing the often-neglected notion of an *intrareligious* dialogue, that is, an inner dialogue within myself, an encounter in the depth of my

*Ezra Pound's translation.

73

personal religiousness, having met another religious experience on that very intimate level. In other words, if *interreligious* dialogue is to be real dialogue, an *intrareligious* dialogue must accompany it; that is, it must begin with my questioning myself and the *relativity* of my beliefs (which does not mean their *relativism)*, accepting the challenge of a change, a conversion, and the risk of upsetting my traditional patterns. *Quaestio mihi factus sum,* "I have made a question of myself," said that great African Augustine. One simply cannot enter the arena of genuine religious dialogue without such a self-critical attitude.

My point is this: I shall never be able to meet the other as the other meets and understands himself or herself if I do not meet and understand her in and as myself. To understand the other as 'other' is, at the least, not to understand her as she understands her-self (which is certainly not as 'other', but as self). Obviously this self that understands the other is not my previous *ego* that reduces the other to my own unchanged self. Each process of real understanding changes me as much as it changes the other. Real understanding transforms my *ego* as well as the *alius.* The meeting point—and this is my thesis—is not a neutral dialectical arena that leaves both of us untouched, but a self that besides being myself is also shared by the other. This is to say, among other things, that I am not advocating any reductionism. I have developed this point elsewhere; here I am only concerned to pave the way for such an approach by dismissing as insufficient a minimalistic attitude without, obviously, falling into the trap of exclusivism.

In a laudable effort to avoid an exclusivist and paternalist posture, some modern writers are tempted by the *phenomenological epochê,* improperly so-called in this context, which is interpreted to be the bracketing of one's 'faith' as the necessary condition for fruitful 'interfaith dialogue'.

This attitude is more common than we usually suppose, although not always under the aegis of so scientific an expression. When a christian, for example, thinks he can understand another religion or be a partner in dialogue without engaging his own religious convictions, he is trying to practice this kind of *epochê.* When a hindu thinks he can genuinely experience another religion just by experimenting, by accepting—for the time being and the sake of the experiment—the rites, practices, and beliefs of the other, he too is intending to bracket his 'faith' by the *epochê* we are discussing. Has the hindu really bracketed his convictions when he claims to follow the christian path for a time? Has the christian shut off his christian faith when he tries to forget his beliefs or preferences and accommodate himself to the forms and habits of another tradition? No one today, I guess, would say that Ramakrishna Paramahamsa or Roberto de Nobili practiced *epochê* when they sincerely tried to enter the heart of another religion. Rather, they were impelled by a belief that their personal religion was wide enough and deep enough to allow such an embrace.

2. CRITIQUE OF THE SO-CALLED PHENOMENOLOGICAL EPOCHÊ IN THE RELIGIOUS ENCOUNTER

I shall offer here only some critical considerations of this attitude without, I hasten to add, tackling just now the many other problems involved in the phenomenology and philosophy of religious dialogue.

Although this chapter seems to have a negative character because it attempts to dispel a misunderstanding, it actually offers a positive standpoint, namely that inner dialogue involving the whole person is the necessary condition for a real and fruitful encounter of religions.

The opinion I am going to criticize understands *epochê* as putting aside one's personal religious convictions, suspending judgment on the validity of one's own religious tenets; in a word, bracketing the concrete beliefs of individual allegiance to a particular confession.

The good intention underlying this attitude is obvious: the *epochê* is put forward in order to prevent undue dominance from any one side or to be able to understand better without bias or prejudice. The *epochê* would thus provide a common ground, a necessary condition for genuine dialogue in which neither side predominates. It is feared that if I approach my partner with strong personal convictions, either I shall not be able to listen to, much less understand, him, her, or it, filled as I am with my own tenets, or that we shall be unable to find a common language.

If I believe in God or Christ or *karma*, for instance, and my partner does not, unless for the sake of dialogue I 'put off' my belief in God, Christ, or *karma*, we shall not be able to establish a real dialogue without privileges on either side. So it is said. The *epochê* procedure has been compared to a kind of methodological doubt. I temporarily suspend my judgment about some fundamental tenets I hold true, bracket my personal 'faith', because I do not want to impose it on my partner nor influence her in the least regarding the contents of our dialogue. Thus I am ready to meet her on her own ground, having renounced my personal standing.

The positive aspect of such an attempt lies in the fact that it distin-

guishes between the conceptualized beliefs of a person and the underlying existential faith. If the subject matter of the *epochê* consists of the concepts we form about a particular idea, then we should be able to perform
and even welcome such an operation. The problem arises when we pretend to bracket not a formulation, a notion, but a fundamental conviction
of the person at the existential level. If we accept the distinction between
faith and belief, we may be able to agree to a certain necessary *epochê* of
our beliefs, but I would prefer to call for transcending them altogether as
long as we are engaged in a serious interreligious dialogue. The *epochê*
looks rather like a closet for temporarily storing one's personal convictions for the sake of the dialogue; whereas transcending our concepts is
not simply a methodological device. A nonconceptual awareness allows
different translations of the same transconceptual reality for different
notional systems without methodological strategies.

The need and the place for a truly phenomenological *epochê* comes in
the introductory stage, getting to know a particular religiousness by
means of an unbiased description of its manifestations.

a. Negative

My contention is that transferring the *epochê* to a field not its own, like that
of ultimate convictions in the interreligious dialogue, would be:
- psychologically impracticable,
- phenomenologically inappropriate,
- philosophically defective,
- theologically weak,
- and religiously barren.

Before taking up the burden of proof, I wish to state emphatically,
although very concisely, that I am not:
- speaking against phenomenology in general or against the phenomenology of religion, which has its own merits and justification,
  because there is room for a clear and valid description of religious
  phenomena;
- attacking authentic phenomenological *epochê* or finding this procedure incorrect in phenomenological analysis;
- belittling all the steps prior and necessary to an interreligious dialogue; human sympathy, for instance, capacity and willingness to
  listen and learn, sincere desire to understand, conscious effort to
  overcome preconceptions, and so on;

- advocating sticking to one's own judgment about the other's religiousness or not performing a phenomenological reduction of my preconceptions regarding the other. I am not saying, for example, that a protestant should from the outset judge a roman catholic idolatrous because of the marian cult.

b. Positive

On the contrary, I am saying that:
- precisely what I should not and cannot put into brackets are my religious convictions, my ultimate religious evaluations, for I must approach religious dialogue without putting my most intimate self on some safe ground outside the confrontation and challenge of the dialogue;
- dialogue is neither teaching nor simply listening; in other words, interreligious dialogue presupposes a rather advanced stage in the confrontation between people of different religious allegiances. Obviously, before meaningful dialogue can take place one must already know the religion of the partner. But one must be both intellectually and spiritually prepared. Dialogue is not mere study or understanding (although, indeed, by dialogue I may well deepen my understanding of my partner), but a total human contrast and participation in deeper communication and fuller communion;
- interreligious dialogue demands a mutual confrontation of everything we are, believe, and believe we are in order to establish that deeper human fellowship without prejudicing the results, without precluding any possible transformation of our personal religiousness.

3. THESIS: THE PHENOMENOLOGICAL 'EPOCHÊ' IS OUT OF PLACE IN THE RELIGIOUS ENCOUNTER

a. Such an *epochê* is *psychologically impracticable* if religious dialogue is to be more than merely doctrinal discussion, in other words, if it is a personal encounter with the whole human being. It would be pretense to affirm that I do not know or am not convinced of my certainties. I cannot simply abstract my deepest convictions or concoct the fiction that I have forgotten or laid aside what I hold to be true. Just this would be required if I really had to bracket my 'faith'.

If for instance I am convinced that God created the world or that the law of *karma* is true, I cannot act (and dialogue is action) *as if* I did not believe in these tenets. Even if I sincerely tried to bracket these convictions, they would go on conditioning and generating a score of side issues. My partner simply would not understand why I maintain the fundamental goodness of this world against empirical evidence or why I see congruences where he does not, and so on. In other words, every reason I might adduce in our discussion regarding the ultimate nature of the world or human behavior would spring from my repressed convictions (the existence of a creator, the validity of the karmic line, and so forth).

Imagine I am reading a detective story. Just when I am at the climax, someone who has read the novel tells me "who done it." I cannot continue reading *as if* I did not know. Not only are the charm, interest, and tension gone, but the reading becomes insipid or at least qualitatively different. If I still read on, my interest will shift to checking plot consistency or, for example, the writer's skill and style.

On the contrary, the genuine phenomenological *epochê* is psychologically possible because it does not engage the entire *psyche*, the whole person; it is an intellectual attitude adopted to get at the phenomenon with the requisite accuracy. I can remain immobile if I like while speaking, but I must open and close my arms to embrace somebody.

b. This method is also *phenomenologically inappropriate*, and this for several reasons:

To ask for the psychological inhibition required to lock up all my religious convictions for the time being—when it is no longer a question of description and understanding but of confrontation and dialogue—is almost an offense against phenomenology, as if the latter feared our psychological constitution. If there is a foe to the now classical phenomenology, it is the so-called psychologism. It could even be said—as the first volume of Husserl's *Logische Untersuchungen* shows— that phenomenology emerges out of the effort to overcome and discard the psychological constituent-aspects of human consciousness. Both the subjective attitude and the objective projection are overcome in phenomenology because they do not belong to the realm of 'transcendental consciousness', the only place where the 'appearance of the essences', of the phenomena, occurs. But dialogue comes only after the transcendental-phenomenological reduction has been used as a methodological device to discover the 'transcendental ego' or 'pure consciousness'.

Submitting religious dialogue to phenomenological analysis—something quite apart from existentially performing the religious dialogue itself—one discovers that if the rule of *epoché* were valid, it should also be applied to the partner's personal convictions so that having thoroughly bracketed both sides, religious dialogue would be impossible. Such an analysis would still detect vestiges of a superiority complex on the part of whoever defends or practices this *epochê:* They think they can accommodate themselves to the mind of the other and put away their own preconceptions, while the partner is not asked to do so. I repeat: The phenomenological *epochê* has its place in the study and initial clarification of religious phenomena, but not in the actual performance of dialogue.

The authentic phenomenological *epochê,* further, does not bracket my convictions or my claim to truth. When dealing with the *noêmata,* the essences given in the 'eidetic intuition', that is, with the manifestation of pure objects in the 'transcendental consciousness', phenomenological investigation brackets the external 'existence' (outside the mind) of the idea described. This makes sense within the Husserlian framework, but extending the *epochê* outside the limits for which it is intended amounts to an unwarranted extrapolation.

Phenomenology, and this is not its least merit, teaches precision in philosophical and prephilosophical investigation. It aims to lay bare the phenomenon so as to have, first, an 'objective' description (as far as possible) and, second, to allow well-founded and justified interpretation. Phenomenology teaches us to listen to the phenomenon and to approach it with a minimum of presuppositions.

Now it is phenomenologically wrong, which amounts to saying it is a methodological error, to leave outside the dialogue an essential part of its subject matter.

In a hindu-christian dialogue on the nature and role of grace, for instance, neither participant can meaningfully lock away—for security or whatever—his personal commitment to and belief in grace. Otherwise the 'dialogue' becomes one partner inspecting the other's opinions, and not a real existential exchange on the religious level.

As an analysis of the conditions for a meaningful *epochê* shows, the very possibility of the *epochê* rests on assumptions that do not exist in many cultures and religious traditions. There are, for example, systems of thought and ways of life that do not make room for such a distinction between my belief and the truth it embodies, much less for a separation between them. To understand what the *epochê* is about, and even more to perform it, a certain sort of mind is required and also to some extent a particular culture, which cannot presume to universality. There are in fact many cultures and religions in which the distinction between the truth and one's conviction of it is not possible, nor between ideas and what they "intend," the formulation and the formulated thing, and so on.

c. This phenomenological *epochê* is *philosophically defective* when applied to religious dialogue.

First of all, cartesian methodological doubt—whatever its other merits—is not applicable here. It would be a philosophical mistake. Nobody, not even a philosopher, can jump over his own shadow. You do not experiment with ultimate convictions. You experience them.

Ultimate convictions—and if they are religious they are ultimate—cannot be bracketed; there is no *doer* left to perform such a maneuver. I have nothing with which to manipulate what is by definition ultimate. Were such manipulation possible, it would mean either total suicide with no resurrection possible or that my ultimate convictions are not ultimate, for beyond them the manipulator would remain pulling the strings.

If I believe in God, for example, I cannot pretend that I do not believe in God or speak and act *as if* there were no God when—by definition if I believe in him—it is God who lets me speak and act. Even methodologically I cannot put him aside when I am convinced that it is he who enables me to deny or bracket him. The 'God' I can dismiss—even for a moment—as an unnecessary hypothesis is undoubtedly not a necessary Absolute.

We can obviously bracket formulations and stop pressing certain points if we 'sense', whatever our motives, that they are not opportune. But the *epochê* in question does not intend to bracket only formulae. In other words, Descartes could very methodically doubt everything but his own method.

Were such an *epochê* maintained, the dialogue would not even reach the level of a philosophical encounter, for philosophy implies and requires a sincere and unconditional search for truth, and there can be no such search if my truth is removed from the sight of my partner, for fear of frightening him with my convictions or out of reverence for him, not wanting to dazzle him with the abundant light I keep for myself.

d. Such a procedure is *theologically weak.* Can I lay down my "faith"—even methodologically or "strategically"—like a hat?

This would imply:

that there is no fundamental understanding possible, no basic human accord unless I distance myself from any type of faith, thus reducing faith to a kind of luxury. Faith would then not be necessary for a full human life because we claim to encounter our fellow-being on the deepest religious level without it.

that my particular faith is so one-sided, so limited, that it represents an obstacle to human understanding, something that must be locked away or banished to some distant chamber of my being if I am to seek universal fellowship with other humans. If I keep my faith in brackets it is doubtlessly because I think it does not foster religious understanding, probably because my partner is not enough advanced to bear the "sublime heights" of my particular brand of faith, which I carefully try to withhold from his scrutiny.

It is not simply a question of human respect—in every sense—but of anthropological integrity. If faith is something a person can discard with impunity so that he can still meet his fellow beings religiously, meaningfully, and humanly, this amounts to affirming that what I happen to believe is simply supererogatory to my being and has no fundamental relevance for my humanity.

e. Finally, such an *epochê* would be *religiously barren:* At a stroke it would delete the very subject matter of the dialogue. If in the religious dialogue I meet a person belonging to another religious tradition, we do not meet just to talk about the weather or merely to discuss some noncommittal doctrinal points, but to speak of her and my own ultimate concerns, about our ultimate convictions, about how we see and understand life, death, God, Man, and so on. If I come to the encounter devoid of any religious commitment, so open and fresh that I have nothing, nothing of my own to contribute—besides the unbearable pretension of such a claim—I shall have frustrated any possible religious dialogue. We should be discussing precisely what I have bracketed. In order not to 'hurt' the other fellow with my convictions (suspicious notion!), I offend her by pretending I can meet her without laying all my cards on the table. How am I going to talk about her? Shall I examine her religious feelings and opinions before the higher tribunal of my uncommitted, unattached, and open attitude? Isn't the very opposite the case? Does this not betray an almost pathological attachment to my 'faith', such a fear of losing it that I dare not risk it, but prefer instead to preserve it under lock and key?

To exclude my religious convictions from religious dialogue is like renouncing the use of reason in order to enter a reasonable encounter.

4. TOWARD A GENUINE RELIGIOUS ENCOUNTER

It is not the purpose of these reflections to elaborate an alternative. To mention the following suggestions suffices:

A religious dialogue must first of all be an authentic *dialogue*, without superiority, preconceptions, hidden motives, or convictions on either side. What is more, if it is to be an authentic dialogue it must also preclude preconceiving its aims and results. We cannot enter a dialogue having already postulated what will come of it or having resolved to withdraw should it enter areas we have a priori excluded. Dialogue does not primarily mean study, consultation, examination, preaching, proclamation, learning, and so on; if we insist on dialogue we should respect and follow its rules. Dialogue listens and observes, but it also speaks, corrects, and is corrected; it aims at mutual understanding.

Second, religious dialogue must be genuinely *religious*, not merely an exchange of doctrines or intellectual opinions, and so it runs the risk of modifying my ideas, my most personal horizons, the very framework of my life. Religious dialogue is not a salon entertainment.

This amounts to saying that dialogue must proceed from the depths of my religious attitude to these same depths in my partner. In other words I understand her, or try to, both from and within my faith, not by putting it aside. How could I possibly comprehend with mere reason something that very often, without necessarily being irrational, claims somehow to be more than sheer rationality?

Imagine we are discussing the meaning and function of sacrifice. Only if I believe, one way or another, in that act or event that makes sacrifice reasonable shall I be able to understand in depth what my partner really believes, and vice versa of course. Otherwise I may pretend I understand him (because I follow his description and know the effects of sacrifice, and so forth), but I shall miss the point of his belief and, in fact, whether I say so or not, most likely regard his belief as pure magic. In brief, the kernel of the purely religious act is phenomenologically undetectable, at least with the theory of phenomenology accepted up to now. I am saying that the *phenomenon* of religion does not exhaust the whole of religious *reality*, so that besides, not opposed to, phenomenology of religion there is yet room for philosophy and theology—and indeed for religion itself.

The peculiar difficulty in the phenomenology of religion is that the religious pisteuma is different from and not reducible to the Husserlian noêma. The pisteuma is that core of religion that is open or intelligible only to a *religious* phenomenology. In other words, the belief of the believer belongs essentially to the religious phenomenon. There is no 'naked' or 'pure' belief separate from the person who believes. This being the case, the noêma of a religiously skeptical phenomenologist does not correspond to the pisteuma of the believer. The religious phenomenon appears only as pisteuma and not as mere noêma. How to reach the pisteuma is an urgent and tantalizing task for religious phenomenology.

We lack a Philosophy of Religion. We have philosophies of religions, that is, philosophies of particular religious traditions, or we have—and this causes difficulty in the religious encounter—the extrapolation of one religion's philosophy to other religious traditions for which it was neither intended nor suitable.

It almost goes without saying that the Philosophy of Religion I anticipate would not reduce all religions to one homogenous pudding. On the contrary, it would allow the most variegated beliefs and religious traditions to flourish in its field, uprooting only isolationism and misunderstanding (not to say resentment and envy) to make room for a healthy and natural pluralism. We will have a true Philosophy of Religion not by lumping everything together, but by discovering our religious root, which grows, flowers, and gives fruit in the most multiform way. Only the walls may fall and private gardens open their gates. . . . Such a philosophy results only from the mystical adventure of seeing truth from within more than one religious tradition. Interreligious dialogue is undoubtedly a preparation for this, a stepping stone to that intrareligious dialogue where living faith constantly demands from us a total renewal, or—in christian terms—a real, personal, and ever-recurring *metanoia*.

6

The Category of Growth in Comparative Religion

A Critical Self-Examination

ὅς γὰρ οὐκ ἔστιν καθ᾽ ἡμῶν
ὑπὲρ ἡμῶν ἔστιν.
Whoever is not against us,
is for us.

—Mk. IX:40 (Lk. IX:50)*

THE ECHO PRODUCED BY SOME OF MY WRITINGS DEALING
with problems in Comparative Religion invites me to restate thematically one of the main issues in the encounter of religions.

*Significantly enough, the Vulgata translated both Mark and Luke: "Qui enim non est adversus *vos*, pro *vobis* est," probably not wanting to contradict Mt. XII:30 ("Qui non est *mecum* contra *me* est") and Lk. XI:23.

This chapter tries to overcome the temptation of self-defense. I shall try to rethink my approach to the problem of the encounter of christian faith with the religions of the world and present it for correction or even total eclipse. How can I put forward more than a hypothesis in this field of open dialogue just now emerging among religions?

Ultimately my aim is not to defend or attack either christianity or any other religion, but to understand the problem. It is precisely because I take seriously Christ's affirmation that he is the way, the truth, and the life[1] that I cannot reduce his significance only to historical christianity. It is because I also take seriously the saying of the Gītā that all action done with a good intention reaches Kṛṣṇa,[2] and the message of the Buddha that he points the way to liberation,[3] that I look for an approach to the encounter of religions that will contain not only a deep respect for but an enlightened confidence in these very traditions—and eventually belief in their messages.

Because I am equally concerned with contemporary Man, only too often wearied by a certain 'religious' inflation when it is a better world for her fellow-beings she wants to build, I cannot consider the meeting of religions exclusively as a problem concerned with the past or relevant only to traditional religions. It speaks to the modern secular individual as well.

1. THE INSUFFICIENT METHODOLOGICAL APPROACHES

One main objection to some of my writings is that I have undertaken a totally 'false method': instead of defending christianity, showing the demonic character of paganism and 'utilizing' the tools of hinduism to proclaim the christian gospel, I involved myself with 'pagan' absurdities, daring to 'interpret' positively pagan texts in a certain way and thus defending 'paganism' instead of undermining it. The reason for this is alleged to be my assumption that Christ is already present in hinduism. In short, I 'interpret' paganism with 'christian concepts', that is, I misinterpret it instead of 'utilizing' it for christian apologetics; or, in the words of a benevolent hindu critic, I do just the opposite: My interpretation of Christ is in fact a hindu interpretation.

But my purpose is not christian or hindu apologetics. I am not concerned with defending one or the other religion, one or the other thesis. This does not mean I am betwixt and between and stand nowhere at all; rather I start from the existential situation where I happen to be. I am not assuming the position of the aseptic-scientific mind beyond good and evil or outside the dilemma that claims to be ultimate. I affirm only that I am starting from my personal situation, without caring at this moment to describe it further. I am not writing on behalf of one or another religious tradition. I am speaking for myself and inviting my contemporaries to sincere dialogue.

Now, and this has been sometimes a cause of misunderstanding, I cannot speak many languages at the same time or defend many fronts simultaneously. External circumstances have led me to write more often for christians—trying to open them up to other religious intuitions—than for hindus or buddhists. Some, contrary to the criticism voiced above, consider this a 'proof' that I am still on the christian side. Others have interpreted this in the opposite way, namely that I believe christians are in more urgent need of that opening to others than hindus and buddhists. Again, I am not defending myself but simply trying to understand.

It seems to me that my deepest divergence from some of my critics is not so much in method as in understanding the fundamental christian fact. Ultimately I would not accept absolutizing christianity in order to consider that its truth has an exclusive claim that monopolizes salvation. In other words, I would not equate historical christianity with transhistorical truth, nor, for that matter, ahistorical hinduism with a historical message. Insofar as it is a historical religion, christianity belongs to history and should not transgress the boundaries of history; insofar as it conveys ahistorical values, hinduism should not be totally identified with a historical religion. I am well aware, of course, that christianity contains more than just a historical message, that the history of salvation implies the salvation of history, and that this latter has an eschatological value transcending history. I am convinced, similarly, that hinduism is also a historical phenomenon and a cultural asset in the history of mankind. Most of the misunderstandings in this field arise from the fact that only too often comparisons are made between heterogeneous elements: We judge one religious tradition from inside and the other from outside. Any vision from within, with belief and personal commitment, includes at once the concreteness (and so the limitations) of that particular religion and the universal truth it embodies. A view from outside cannot see this link and judges only by objectified values. But religion, by definition— that is, as what it claims to be—is not completely objectifiable, nor is it reducible to mere subjectivity.

For this reason I do not accept the *utilization-interpretation* dilemma, nor do I find that these approaches do justice to the dialogue among religions toward which we are today impelled.

The difference between an exposition of christian mysteries *utilizing* indian or other concepts and images on the one hand and an *interpretation* of the religions of the world by means of christian concepts on the other would be important were I engaged in the defense of a particular doctrine. But for one who sincerely strives to find and express the truth, for one who does not discard either hindu or christian tradition as demonic, the difference is not relevant. Indeed, someone who humbly desires to make a radical investigation cannot take as his starting point a position that fundamentally and inexorably begs the question. I do not think either christian or hindu has to start with a kind of entrenched a priori that makes any meeting and dialogue impossible from the outset.

I am not considering whether or not what Christ conveyed is the same message hinduism conveys. I am, however, making a fundamental assumption: The *ultimate* religious *fact* does not lie in the realm of doctrine or even individual self-consciousness. Therefore it can—and may well—be present everywhere and in every religion, although its 'explicitation' may require varied degrees of discovery, realization, evangelization, revelation, hermeneutics, and so on. This makes it plausible that this fundamental—religious—*fact* may have different names, interpretations, levels of consciousness, and the like that are not irrelevant but that may be existentially equivalent for the person undergoing the concrete process of realization.

In a word, I am pleading for the *dekerygmatization* of faith. The kerygma—like the myth—has its place within any religion, but the 'proclamation of the message' should not be identified without qualifications with the reality religions aim to disclose. I would apply this in a very special way to christianity, and I may also say my reason for this is a conviction that the living and ultimately the real Christ is not the kerygma of the Lord, but the Lord himself. The naked Christ means also the 'dekerygmatized' Christ.

I would say there is a primordial theandric fact that appears with a certain fullness in Jesus,[4] but that is equally manifested and at work elsewhere. This is the Mystery that exists since the beginning of time and will appear only at the end of time in its 'capital' fullness.[5] It is in my opinion a disheartening 'microdoxy' to monopolize that mystery and make it the private property of christians.

The main difference between 'interpretation' and 'utilization' then seems to lie in this:

The *utilization* of, say, greek or hindu concepts to expound christian doctrine implies that I know well what christian belief is and that I *use* some thought-patterns from an external source to expound christian doctrine.

The *interpretation* of, say, hinduism or greek religion along christian lines implies that I know well what hinduism and greek religion are and that I interpose some thought patterns coming from an external source (christianity) in order to explain those very religions.

Let us now analyze these two methodological approaches to the encounter of religions, *utilization* and *interpretation*. It is my contention that these two methods are not valid methods for a fruitful encounter of religions. Moreover, they seem to be incompatible with at least a significant part of the christian attitude. Further, I shall contend that only the category of growth does justice to the real religious situation of our time.

a. Utilization

Time and again it is said that the proper christian attitude in the encounter of religions is that demonstrated by the christian Fathers themselves: *utilizing* the elements of pre-christian thought to expound christian doctrine. Undoubtedly this has been an opinion held by christians and by people of other religions as well.

To begin with, historical evidence for the first generation of christians utilizing already existing elements of thought merely to express their own christian ideas as their main or only procedure is very questionable, and, although this may sometimes have been the method, it was never the creative nor the prevailing attitude in christianity. History shows that precisely where the christian message succeeded in transforming a society it was never by such a 'utilization', but, on the contrary, by its being assimilated—the christian word is *incarnated*—by that particular religion and culture, the christian fact being the leaven.

Very often indeed, we cannot say whether the Fathers of the Church were 'utilizing', or just the opposite, and in fact much of the polemics and tension in the Patristic period are due precisely to the coexistence of both processes: that of 'utilizing' and that of being utilized. Were Plato's ideas christianized or was christianity 'platonized'? Were Aristotle's concepts of *ousia* and the like utilized for the christian doctrine of the Trinity, or did the christian idea of the Trinity evolve as it did due to the internal dialectic of the concepts thus introduced? To put it differently, is not a great part of what is today called christian doctrine or even christianity precisely the result of such a symbiosis?

'Christian doctrine' did not come out of nothing but was the expression of certain beliefs within a specific thought-pattern, which, in the beginning, was either 'jewish' or 'gentile' (this word embracing more than one cultural form), but certainly not christian. No christian doctrine of the Trinity nor any Christology existed before its expression in gentile or jewish categories. The christian experience—belief or whatever one wishes to call it, but assuredly not doctrine—was molded, found expression—in a word, became doctrine— by means of already existing thought-patterns. It could not be otherwise. The first christians did not 'utilize' greek or other thought-categories of the times in order to convey what had not yet found expression. On the contrary, only by means of these categories—jewish and gentile—could the christian experience be expressed and understood at all. A cogent proof for this is the significant fact that orthodox and heretical views in the Trinitarian and Christological controversies of that age both used the terminology of their respective milieux. Thus, to say 'three *ousiai*' or 'three *hypostáseis*' (substances) meant one thing to Origen and another to Arius, or to say 'three *prosopa*' (persons) meant one thing to Hippolytus and another to Sabellius. They were not utilizing greek concepts to express one single christian intuition, but they had a different understanding of the christian fact, perhaps because they were carried away by the very concepts they used. One could almost say they were utilized, used by those very concepts.

In fact, greek concepts handled (and often mishandled) the christian event. Saint John, for instance, did not utilize (and transform) the Philonic concept of Logos to convey his 'message'; it was almost the other way around: the Logos took flesh, I would say—begging not to be misunderstood—not only in the womb of Mary, but also in the midst of the intellectual speculation on the Logos at that time. To use utterly new words and expressions to say what Christ was all about would have been unintelligible—and impossible. To give expression to the christian faith not by dint of willful and calculated utilization but through a natural, cultural, and spiritual process, the only possibility was—and always is—to let it take form, name, and flesh in terms of the contemporary culture. In scholastic terms: The logical analogy of the concepts, necessary for their intelligibility outside their univocal realm, implies also an ontological analogy. If the Johannine concept of Logos were not somehow analogous to the pre-christian concept, if it did not start from an interpretation of a concept already existing, it could neither be intelligible nor in any way 'inspired'. A parallel example would be that of the Buddha interpreting the already existing concept of *nirvāṇa* in a new and original way.

But one may retort that the situation is different today: There *are* dogmas; there *is* a Church. There is now a definite christian doctrine and even a so-called 'christian thought'. But, it is further said, such 'thought' can very well profit from concepts and ideas borrowed from other cultures and religions. This we may grant for the sake of the argument, but we should emphasize that such a method of borrowing will never go very deep or lead us very far; it will touch only the surface and lead to an artificial and decidedly shallow adaptation. There will emerge from it neither synthesis nor symbiosis, nor even a serious confrontation. It will all remain foreign and external, mere superstructure.

That there is now an elaborate christian thought-system makes it all the more urgent to overcome the danger of isolation and self-satisfaction by reaching out to meet other religious traditions, learning from them, and interpreting them in the light of one's own beliefs. Two main reasons seem relevant here. The first is the almost self-evident fact that the western christian tradition seems to be exhausted, I might almost say effete, when it tries to express the christian message in a meaningful way for our times. Only by cross-fertilization and mutual fecundation may the present state of affairs be overcome; only by stepping over present cultural and philosophical boundaries can christian life again become creative and dynamic. Obviously this applies to the other religions as well: It is a two-way traffic. The encounter of religions today is vital for the religious life of our contemporary time; otherwise, traditional religions will remain altogether obsolete, irrelevant relics of the past, and what is worse, we will be uprooted and impoverished.

The time for one-way traffic in the meeting of cultures and religions is, at least theoretically, over, and if there are still powerful vestiges of a past colonialistic attitude, they are dying out by the very fact that they become conscious. Neither monologue nor conquest is tenable. The *spolia aegyptiorum* mentality is today no longer possible or in any way justifiable. To think that one people, one culture, one religion has the right—or the duty for that matter—to dominate all the rest belongs to a past period in world history. Our contemporary degree of consciousness and our present-day conscience, East and West, finds, by and large, such a pretension utterly untenable. The meeting point is neither my house nor the mansion of my neighbor, but the crossroads outside the walls, where we may eventually decide to put up a tent—for the time being.[6]

Finally, there is a theoretical point to consider: If the use of a concept foreign to a given cultural setup is to be made viable, if it is to be grafted successfully onto another system of thought (the christian, for example),

it will succeed because it has somehow attained a certain homogeneity
with the host cultural and religious world so that it may live there. If this
is the case, it amounts to recognizing that its possible use depends on a
certain previous homogeneity, on a certain presence of the one meaning
within the other framework; otherwise it would be completely impossible
to utilize the concept in question. In spite of the heterogeneity between the
greek and christian conception of the Logos, for instance, the former had
to offer a certain affinity with the new meaning that would be enhanced
once it was assumed. In other words, 'utilization', even if it is admitted as
a proper procedure, can be fruitful only if based on a previous relatedness
that is the condition for its use. Only homogeneous materials can be used
if any integration is to survive. The real problem, thus, lies deeper—and
elsewhere.

b. Interpretation

Some critics maintain that it is quite wrong in the encounter of religions
(at least from the christian point of view) to interpret the texts and statements of other religious traditions in light of the christian intuition.

   If the faith of the christian were totally foreign to such traditions, if
the christian fact had nothing to do with the fundamental religious fact
or human reality in its ultimate concern, then obviously to introduce a
hermeneutical principle (the christian one) completely alien to those traditions would be unwarranted. But this is not necessarily a christian
position.

   Be this as it may, I would offer the following condensed remarks.

   First, one could also question here the historical accuracy of the statement that authentic christians never interpreted pre-christian religions
but only utilized them for their own kerygma. I wonder then what it was
Saint Paul did with the jewish Bible if not interpret it, and rather drasti-
cally at that. Moreover, most of the Church Fathers and the Scholastics
undoubtedly did this very thing vis-à-vis 'nonchristian' thinkers and
greek concepts; that is, they interpreted them according to what they
thought to be the christian line of development. In this way the traditional
doctrine of the *sensus plenior* was developed: the fuller meaning of pre-
christian ideas seen in the light of Christ. This idea underlies nothing less
than the incorporation of the Old Testament into christianity.

   Second, the question becomes even clearer if we consider that ultimately we cannot use a concept without at the same time interpreting it in
a certain way. If Saint Paul, for instance, had 'utilized' a stoic or gnostic

concept of *soma* (body) without interpreting it in his own way, this would have amounted to accepting fully its stoic or gnostic connotations. The work of polishing or emphasizing or even sometimes twisting, which theologians of every age have always done: What is this if not simply interpreting or, I would say, reinterpreting already existing concepts?

Third, the main objection to a christian interpretation of the religions of the world seems to rest on a double assumption: on the idea that all that does not belong "officially" and "visibly" to historical christianity or to the Church is sin and satanic (an extrapolation of the saying that everything not born of God is sin[7]) and on the fear that such an interpretation would mean recognizing that the Spirit of God has also been at work in other religious traditions[8] and that even Christ, who is before Abraham,[9] is somehow present and effective in those other religions. (Lord, we have seen some performing miracles in your name who do not belong to our group. . . .[10] "The rock indeed was Christ!"[11])

I personally cannot subscribe to any opinion that monopolizes God, Logos, Christ, and even Jesus and sets the rules for how the kingdom of God must work. I disagree from a purely human standpoint, as well as from scientific, theological, and christian points of view. There were zealots even among the Apostles, but Christ was not a zealot.

Finally, there remains the objection from the other side, that is, from the followers of other religious traditions. Are they going to be satisfied with a christian interpretation?

One may answer, first of all, that these religions are going to be satisfied even less by the other method, which simply uses their own tools to preach something apparently contrary to their traditions and beliefs. Yet the force of the argument clearly does not come from this quarter.

The one reason underlying resistance to a christian interpretation seems to be that, with few exceptions, Christ has been considered the monopoly of christians, as if Christ were *ad usum delphini,* solely for the benefit of orthodox believers. So when one mentions even the name of Christ, other religions understand it in a polemical or at least foreign way.

Now, it is clear that any genuine 'christian' interpretation must be valid and true, and for this very reason it must also be acceptable to those who are being interpreted, a basic methodological rule for any interpretation. This means that no interpretation of any religion is valid if the followers of that religion do not recognize it as such. But this means also, by the same token, that nobody can propose as christian something that christians do not recognize as such. On the other hand the history of religious traditions is not closed, and it shows that certain ideas or conceptions denounced as heretical at a given moment were accepted later on. In point of fact the evolution—and, as I am going to say, the growth—of any religion has been brought about mainly by 'foreign' ideas incorporated into the body of beliefs.

Further, there is still another, though ambivalent, reason for the 'christian interpretation' or any interpretation of one religion by another, for that matter. I may point out the pro and the contra.

Pro. If the christian interpretation of, say, *karma* is to be a valid one, as has already been said, it has to be valid for the two traditions. This is to say that such an interpretation will have to have reached a depth where the one tradition does not find it deformed and the other one finds it acceptable. Obviously the new interpretation, because of its incorporation into christianity, may find some shades of meaning that hindus and buddhists may not accept, but provided that they recognize the starting interpretation as a legitimate one, nothing stands in the way of the new step.

Contra. Religions are organic wholes and each particular tenet makes sense within the entire body of doctrine. Now to transplant one particular notion into another body is not only a delicate operation, but it also requires a homogeneous body to receive it. Otherwise what we have done is to get stimulated by the "foreign" tenet, but in fact we have not crossed the boundaries of one tradition. This is particularly visible with the very words we use. Words are meaningful within a context and mere translation may not do. In other terms, not everything is susceptible of an exogenous interpretation.

Here we must confess that a great deal of fundamental work has still to be done. I would like now to state tentatively the direction in which I would be inclined to look for further research.

2. PHILOSOPHIES AND PHILOSOPHY OF RELIGION

One fact should be clearly and sincerely acknowledged: Considering the geographical and historical coordinates of our times, we do not have a Philosophy of Religion worthy of the name. What is termed *philosophy of religion* is usually a particular philosophy of a particular religion expressed in more or less vague or universal terms and then applied almost a priori to all other 'religions' of the world. Undoubtedly mankind can be considered a unity, and from the reflection of a particular group one may sometimes draw conclusions that are valid for the entire human race, but this approximate method is distinctly insufficient as a working and effective Philosophy of Religion for our times. Even if in the past such efforts were made, the worldview that prompted such attempts has been superseded today when the whole earth—for good or ill— begins to form a geographical and historical unit for the first time in human existence.

The fact that traditional religions are mainly oriented to the past, for instance, and that the religious vitality of mankind has produced new forms of religiousness marginal to, if not in conflict with, traditional religions is part of the same problem: namely, we do not have a Philosophy of Religion. Ideologies and other secular forms that claim a total hold on the human person, and thereby the right to direct his life, are numberless in our times. Morphologically, in fact, they are religions, but few would so call themselves because the very name has fallen into widespread disrepute.

Our main point follows. We may easily agree that one cannot envision even the possibility of a Philosophy of Religion without the internal experience peculiar to religion. In terms of classical christian scholasticism, theology is a *charisma,* and faith is required for a real and creative theologian—and here the philosophical and the theological activity should not be artificially severed.

Now, in spite of the claim of every religion to touch the very core of the human being, the 'experience of religion' does not exist. What is given is a religious experience within one particular context, or we may also grant that there is a peculiar internal experience of or within *a* particular religion. Religion in general does not exist.

This would justify *a* philosophy of *a* religion, but not Philosophy of Religion. Either then we agree it is possible internally and authentically to experience more than one religion or we renounce forever a Philosophy of Religion valid for the different world religions; or else, as is generally the case today, Philosophy of Religion is merely replaced by phenomenology of religions—and even then the problem is not solved, as we shall see in the following chapter.

We in no way belittle phenomenology of religion, which has earned much merit in recent times, but to consider it a substitute for Philosophy of Religion would be a serious mistake. *Suum cuique.*

I am not maintaining here that no Philosophy of Religion is possible without the specific 'theological' *charisma* in the scholastic sense. Whatever conception of philosophy (or theology if we prefer) we may have, only a philosophy or theology of religion that takes into account the facts, categories, and intuitions of a particular religion is able and entitled to handle the phenomena of that religion. But for this we must know such data not merely by hearsay but through a genuine effort to understand. Even the strictest philosophical positivism is no exception to this. If, as this latter will tell us, Philosophy of Religion is only the scientific analysis of religious language, one must nevertheless know the particular language, which originated from assumptions rather different, perhaps, than the language of the positivist philosopher himself. In brief, it is not only a question of proper translation; we need a common symbolics not only to check the translation and establish two-way communication, but also even to make the translation. In order to say "'table' means 'Tisch'" I need another common term of reference (my finger, my eyes, and so on) that is able to transfer (translate) the meaning.

Philosophy of Religion is only made possible by a prior philosophy of religions. Only after this, which is more than just a digest of philosophies of religions, will we be on the way to a Philosophy of Religion capable of fulfilling the task that falls to such a discipline today. To elaborate a Philosophy of Religion we need to take religions seriously and, further, to experience them from within, to believe, in one way or another, in what these religions say. Otherwise, we remain floating on the surface. To know what a religion says, we must understand what it says, but for this we must somehow believe in what it says. Religions are not purely objectifiable data; they are also and essentially personal, subjective. As we have said, the particular belief of the believer belongs essentially to religion. Without that belief no philosophy of religions is possible. Merely to describe the tenets or practices the followers of a particular religion claim to acknowledge is not yet philosophy of religions, much less Philosophy of Religion. Needless to say this is only a necessary precondition or requirement, insufficient by itself for a critical Philosophy of Religion.

This seems to be a major challenge in our times; lacking an authentic Philosophy of Religion we shall be able to understand neither the different world religions nor the people and cultures of this earth, for religion is the soul of a culture and one of the most important factors in shaping the human character individually and collectively. Undoubtedly the extrapolation of a particular philosophy into fields beyond the scope of its original application is no longer justifiable.

Yet in fact this still happens in many philosophical, theological, and religious quarters. Christianity is perhaps the religion that has been most concerned with the problem, and yet not only does it not possess any Philosophy of Religion, but it continues to extrapolate all unawares. When, for instance, Saint Paul speaks about the gentiles or the idolators, he has in mind the people of Corinth or Asia Minor or those whom he considers for whatever reason to warrant the name. To apply the jew-gentile dichotomy outside its sphere and call 'gentile' the hindus and buddhists (and even, for that matter, muslims!) is an unwarranted extrapolation, to say the least. Biblical scholarship today does not insist that the entire planet was under water in Noah's time or in utter darkness at the Crucifixion of Christ. It has set geographical boundaries to those statements, but it still has not sufficiently examined the anthropological, metaphysical, and religious boundaries of the Old and New Testaments.

Is such an enterprise, a Philosophy of Religion possible? I believe it cannot be affirmed a priori that it is impossible, although it may remain only an ideal. Philosophy can encompass more than one religion because one can have an authentic internal religious experience in more than one religious tradition without betraying any of them, and of course without confusing genuine experience with artificial experiment. One cannot experiment with religions as if they were rats or plants, but one can believe in them as authentic paths and try to understand and eventually to integrate more than one religious tradition. After all, most of mankind's great religious geniuses did not create or found new forms of religiousness out of nothing; rather they fused more than one religious stream, molding them with their own prophetic gifts. But one need not be a prophet or a founder of a religion to be creative in this new field of research; the philosopher of religion needs, however, to be a believer and to be sufficiently humble and ready to undergo with his faith not an experiment but an experience.

I have said that a philosophy of religion is not impossible but should have added immediately one condition. This condition links us again with the traditional philosophical or theological activity in contradistinction to the individualistic character of western modernity. This condition is, in old parlance, the scholastic (in sense of school), corporate, or ecclesial character of the philosophical enterprise. In present-day terms we may prefer to speak of the dialogical character of Philosophy of Religion.

A genuine Philosophy of Religion in our times, if it is to maintain the claim to speak about the religious dimension of Man, has to be critically aware that neither a single individual nor any single religious tradition has access to the universal range of the human experience. It must then pull together the findings, experiences, and data coming from the four directions of the earth: It has to be dialogical and, like a net, encompass the different religious experiences of humanity.

The main thing favoring such an enterprise is not the individual's psychological capacity to experience sincerely more than one religious tradition, but the fact that there exists something like a fundamental religiousness, a constitutive religious dimension in us, an inbuilt religious or basically human factor, whatever we may care to call it. Surely no religious tradition today takes such hold of the entire human being that it leaves no room for communication and dialogue. Man indeed transcends historical and cultural boundaries.

Human nature is meta-ontologically one. This allows the possibility of an experience that certainly implies overcoming the actual boundaries of a particular religion, without its betrayal.

3. THE VITAL ISSUE: GROWTH

Earlier we said that neither the *use* of a foreign tradition to enrich another one nor the *interpretation* of one religion in the light of another is adequate or appropriate to the philosophical task and the religious need of our times. I submit that the one category able to carry the main burden in the religious encounter and in the further development of religion (and religions) is *growth*. Theology or philosophy, and religion even more, are not simply matters of archaeological interest, nor is religion mainly directed to the past. On the contrary, the future, hope, eschatology, the end of human life, and the world are fundamental religious categories. Religion is equally inclined toward the future, full of that *epektasis* of the greek christian Patristic writings, that is, that attitude of more than expectation, of constantly leaning toward our transhuman or superhuman end. In the life of religion as in the life of a person, where there is no growth there is decay; to stop is stagnation and death.

It would be wrong and methodologically false to restrict the theological task to just imitating the elders. Obviously it is a risky adventure to start towards the *terra incognita* of a really new land in religious consciousness and proceed by discovering new paths. "Men of Galilee, what are you doing here just gazing at the skies? . . ."[12]

After much effort and many painful misunderstandings, christian theology has accepted as fact what in certain theological circles is called the development of dogma. This seems to be a good starting point, but it would hardly suffice if interpreted merely as a kind of explication of something already there. Were religious consciousness static, our task would be only to unfold what was already there nicely 'folded'. There is, however, undoubtedly a development in religious consciousness. Two points should be made immediately in this connection. First, religious consciousness is something more than an external development of a knowing organ that at a certain moment discovers something of which it was not previously aware. Also, because religious consciousness is an essential part of religion itself, the development of this consciousness means the development of religion itself. Second, it amounts to more than just a development in personal consciousness; at the very least human consciousness is set in evolution. What develops, in fact, is the entire cosmos, all creation, reality. The whole universe expands. In a word, there is real growth in Man, in the World, and, I would also add, in God, at least inasmuch as neither immutability nor change are categories of the divine. The divinity is constant newness, pure act as the scholastics said.

So there is not only a development of dogma; there is also a real development of consciousness. We may—or may not—have a system of thought sufficiently elaborated to express this fact adequately, but it is one thing to endure the limitation of the human mind struggling to find proper expression and another thing to dismiss an intuition because it is still in the throes of birth, still a *concipiendum* and not yet a *conceptum*. After all, what is born into life here on earth already complete? Only something already dead, stillborn. As is often remarked, only dead languages do not tolerate mistakes (nobody left to accept them), but a living language has ample place for today's mistakes, which may become tomorrow's rule. The physical theory of an expanding universe may furnish a fair image of what happens in the ontological realm as well.

Without allowing for such growth, no religious maturity is possible. But here growth does not mean only linear development. In spite of every christian theological contrivance, the jewish point of view is quite right when it judges not only Paul but Christ too as real innovators. Given this perspective, the members of the Sanhedrin were not so wrong in condemning Jesus. They really understood what it was all about: not merely evolution, reform, or improvement, but a real mutation, a new step, another sphere, more akin to revolution than to evolution. It is almost a platitude to say that if Jesus were to come to earth now, the Church would put him to death. I interpret this not to mean that the Church has betrayed the message of Jesus (this is not my point now) but that Christ would introduce another revolution, another step, a new wine that he would not allow to be poured into old skins.[13] This constant growth should be a fundamental element of sacramental theology, especially of the liturgical Eucharist.

Growth is perhaps the most pertinent category to express this situation, which is more than simple development or explication. In growth

there is continuity as well as novelty, development as well as a real assimilation of something that was outside and is now incorporated, made one
body. In growth, there is freedom. Perhaps nowhere else is human freedom more visible and more magnificent than in the consciousness of the
religious person who discovers that he or she is the co-creator, the shaper
and builder not only of his or her own life but also of the life of the cosmos: Man is the artist of the mystical body, the free agent who may let
himself and the world go one way or another, who may lead history in one
or another direction. Nothing is more fascinating than the religious existence seen and lived as such a dynamism.

I repeat: Growth means continuity and development, but it also
implies transformation and revolution. Growth does not exclude mutation; on the contrary, there are moments even in the biological realm when
only a real mutation can account for further life. We know roughly the law
of growth for a plant or for a child's body; we do not know, and in a way
we cannot know, the ways growth may possibly grow further. The future
is not just a repetition of the past. (I hope one result of the landing on the
moon will be to liberate us from provincial horizons and foreshortened
views.) How hinduism needs to grow or how christianity or modern
humanism has to grow we may not yet know. The prophet's function is
not precisely to know in advance but to point out the direction and to go
ahead, to ascend the ladder of time, space, and the spirit. There are false
prophets, indeed, but for the same reason that there is false silver and not,
so far, false earth or water; we only falsify things worth falsifying.

Growth does not exclude rupture and internal or external revolution.
We know what the growth of an adolescent means only once the evolution
is complete. We do not know where we are going. Yet in this common
ignorance genuinely religious people experience real fellowship and fra-
ternal communion.

Growth does not deny a process of death and resurrection; quite the
contrary. If growth is to be genuine and not merely a cancer, it implies a
negative as well as a positive metabolism, death as well as a new life. That
we must constantly kill the idols that creep in from all sides, this we are
prepared to accept; we also know that the prophets' lot is to be crushed
between the temple and the palace. It seems, at least to me, an empirical
truth that *metanoia* is the first condition for sound growth and real life.

But what about islām, hinduism, christianity? I am tempted to give
the answer Jesus gave to a similar question put by Peter: "If it should be
my will that he wait until I come, what is that to you? You follow me!"[14]

In the contemporary scene where everything is in the fires of revision and reform, in which every value is contested and the *metanoia* almost total, the authentically religious person cannot shut himself off, close his ears and eyes, and simply gaze toward heaven or brood over the past; he cannot ignore his fellow human beings and act as if religion has assured him that he has no more to learn, nothing to change. He must throw himself into the sea and begin to walk, even if his feet falter and his heart fails.[15] Who are we to stifle the growing seed, to choke humble and personal buds, to quench the smoking wick?[16]

4. BIBLIOGRAPHICAL NOTE

Besides the more than one hundred book reviews scattered among specialized journals and the discussion that took place (over a period of several years) in the Bombay Weekly *The Examiner* (from 1965 onward), cf.:

D. Reetz, "Raymond Panikkar's Theology of Religion," *Religion and Society* (Bangalore, September 1968): 3, pp. 32–54; D.C. Mulder, "Raymond Panikkar's Dialog Met Het Hindoeïsme," *Gereformeers Theologisch Tiydschrift* (August 1969), pp. 186–98; and F. Molinario, "L'evangelizzazione della cultura e delle religione nella sperienza e negli scritti di R. Panikkar," *Testimonianza* (No. 144, 1972).

Regarding specific points, cf. the author's answers to:

J.A. Cuttat, "Vergeistigungs 'Technik' und Umgestaltung in Christus," *Kairos* (Salzburg, 1/1959), pp. 18–30; P. Hacker, "Magie, Gott, Person und Gnade in Hinduismus," *Kairos* (Salzburg, 4/1960), pp. 225–33; and K. Rudolph, "Die Problematik der Religionswissenschaft als akademisches Lehrfach," *Kairos* (Salzburg, 1/1967), pp. 22–42 (all of which may be found in *Kairos* [Salzburg, 1/1960], p. 45 et seq.; [2/1961], pp. 112–14; and [1/1968], pp. 56–67 respectively).

As for the negative criticism these pages have tried to meet without polemics, cf. the article-review by P. Hacker of the author's *Kultmysterium in Hinduismus und Christentum* in *Theologische Revue*, nr. 6 (1967), pp. 370–78, and also Hacker's short essay "Interpretation und 'Benutzung'," 'Kleine Beitrage' in *Zeitschrift für Missionswissenschaft und Religionswissenschaft* 51:3 (Juli 1967), pp. 259–63.

NOTES

1. Cf. Jn. XIV:6.
2. Cf. BG IX, 26–34.
3. Cf. *Saṁyutta-nikāya* V, 421–23.
4. Col. I:19.
5. Cf. 1 Cor. II:7; Eph. I:9–10.
6. Cf. Mk. IX:5.
7. Cf. Rom. XIV:23.
8. Rom. X:10.
9. Jn. VIII:58.
10. Lk. IX:49; Mk. IX:38.
11. 1 Cor. X:4.
12. Acts I:11.
13. Lk. V:37–38.
14. Jn. XXI:22.
15. Mt. XIV:28 sq.
16. Mt. XII:20; cf. Is. XLII:3.

7

Ecumenical Ecumenism

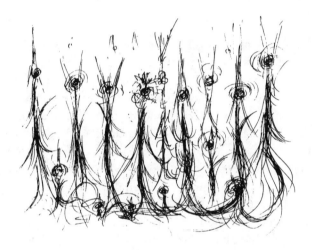

ANY SERIOUS THEOLOGICAL REFLECTION TODAY CONFRONTS
us with ecumenical problems. We can no longer do theology in isolation or only within our 'own' group. Ecumenism is said to be in crisis
nowadays. Perhaps it has lost its novelty, but it could also be that it
requires a more catholic perspective. The human predicament today
requires an extension and transformation of the meaning of the word
"ecumenism." Forty years ago I proposed the term "ecumenical ecumenism" to describe the genuine and sincere encounter of religions, following certain tendencies in christian ecumenism.

Christian ecumenism tries to reach a unity among christians without
stifling their diversity. It does not wish to be a contest that tallies winners
and losers. The goal is always a new point of agreement, in deeper loyalty
to a principle both transcendent and immanent to the various christian

confessions, and because of the recognition of this transcendence-immanence, agreement does not entail uniformity of opinions; it means harmony of enlightened hearts.

Ecumenical ecumenism attempts to extend this new openness to the entire human family. The goal is a better understanding, corrective criticism, and eventually mutual fecundation among the religious traditions of the world, without diluting their respective heritages or prejudging their possible harmony or eventual irreducible differences. The task is still ahead of us, but already some fruits can be seen ripening.

Ecumenical ecumenism has a twofold meaning, both christian and ecumenical:

a. Christian ecumenism, if it is really to be ecumenical, cannot be reduced to settling christian family feuds, as it were, or healing old wounds. It has also to take into account the entire world situation and try to find the place of the religions of the world in the 'christian economy of salvation', without any a priori subordination of other religions to the christian self-understanding. This can be done without watering down this latter christian sense of identity. No true self-understanding precludes another, even *objectively* contradictory, self-understanding, for Man is not only an object of interpretation. Even the position of those christians who make an *Absolutheitsanspruch* for themselves does not contradict the fact that other believers sustain a similar claim to absoluteness. 'You' cannot believe at the same time in both claims, but 'you' and 'we' can believe in the respective claims without contradiction—unless beliefs are totally objectifiable propositions having nothing to do with the believer. In this case the quarrel would be purely philosophical. We would no longer be dealing with beliefs.

A by-product of this ecumenical attitude is that it affords the best setting for the right perspective, even in merely christian controversies. Catholics and protestants would more easily discover their different contexts and understand each other more fully, for instance, when dealing with the nature of the sacraments if they tried to understand also the nature of the hindu *saṁskāra* instead of arguing only from their respective traditional standpoints. The reason is not strategical. It is basically methodological. When seen against a wider and common horizon, divergences and common perspectives appear. In order to understand 'the problem' that together we are trying to investigate, we need to understand our various standpoints. But for this we have to situate the standpoints within a larger background, which is the one offered by the context of the other religion.

b. Ecumenical ecumenism would be the way for the religions of the world to enter into a multivoiced dialogue. I would call it *dharma-samanvaya* or harmonization (convergence, coming together) of all *dharma* or religions, that is, of all traditions dealing with human ultimacy. I repeat that *samanvaya* does not have to mean sameness, but it conveys the hope that today's cacophony may be converted into a symphony tomorrow.

Christians should not shun participating in this ecumenical round-table. They have been pioneers in modern ecumenism, as they have also distinguished themselves in intolerance and exclusivism. Both the positive and the negative experiences are an invaluable contribution. Ecumenical ecumenism represents the common search for truth in a genuine dialogical (not just dialectical) attitude in which religious traditions open not only to one another but also to any other possible dimension of immanence and/or transcendence.

The basic premise of ecumenical ecumenism is that no one individual or collectivity has universal awareness. Awareness dawns with the discovery of the other: no other, no awareness. Whether the other encountered is the physical environment (science), the metaphysical realm (religion), or other people and their works (humanities), human awareness can only be stillborn unless and until it begins to assimilate this fundamental polarity. Yet we have a tendency to construct for ourselves an increasingly uninhabitable world broken into combat zones between "us" and "them." The very word *ecumene* should be redeemed from its ethnocentric connotations.

This either/or mentality seems to be at the root of the current human malaise, and obviously religions, which deal with ultimate problems, are especially sensitive to the kind of exclusivism that condemns the other. We should distinguish here between 'relativism' which is agnostic and untenable and 'relativity,' which is realistic and takes into account that truth itself is relational. On the existential level it is the question of how people and peoples are to relate constructively to one another. It is the most pressing, and often the most studiously avoided, human question of our day. It should not be necessary to evoke the specter of world famine and nuclear weapons to make this point clear. It is obvious that we need to draw upon the strengths of all the traditions of humankind in order to surmount this impasse.

With a view, then, to rendering ecumenism truly ecumenical, the following points should prove useful:

1. Humans are nonachieved, nonfinite, and, in this sense, in-finite beings. They are in the process of becoming something which they are not yet. This process is constitutive, and thus the ideal is not to bring it to an end but to convert dialectical tensions into creative polarities. Thus, the ecumenical task is infinite; it is never finished and never should be finished, for it is a constitutive part of the human pilgrimage. The image of the 'one shepherd and one fold', to use christian idiom, is an eschatological one. Humility is an intellectual virtue. The dialectic of means and ends does not apply here because the 'ends' coalesce with the 'means'. Understanding the other—which is not possible without love—is not a means to anything (to win the other over, for instance) but an end in itself. True ecumenism has a contemplative dimension. This is also why genuine ecumenism has no preconceived ideas or hidden agendas. It is not apologetics. The more we are convinced of our opinions, the more we are defeated by the mystery that overwhelms us.

2. Religions claim to be ways leading people to their fulfilment—however this goal is interpreted or however the way is envisaged: heaven, happiness, justice, liberation, *nirvāṇa,* Reign of God, and so forth. A religion is that set of practices and/or doctrines (orthopraxis is surely as important as orthodoxy) that one *believes* will lead to the liberation or fulfilment of one's being.

3. No religion, ideology, culture, or tradition can reasonable claim to exhaust the universal range of human experience or even the total manifestation of the Sacred. Thus *pluralism,* as distinct from the mere coexistence of a *plurality* of worldviews, becomes today the paramount human and religious imperative. It thus precludes the attempt at domination by any master perspective or absolutely privileged standpoint. Pluralism does not call for a superideology or a supersystem. It implies an almost mythical confidence that other perspectives are also plausible or, more correctly, a mystical respect for the other that authenticates one's own religious experience. Evil and error are not excluded but are robbed of the sting of absoluteness; they are contextualized.

4. All human enterprises of this sort, whether called religions, ideologies, humanisms, atheisms, or the like, are engaged in this struggle for human fullness, even if they understand this notion differently, to the point sometimes of appearing to outsiders as merely animal or in-human

or super-human. We may and even must endeavor to put our point across and defend it. Thus, encounter and dialogue between these ways of life become imperative. Here one should carefully distinguish the merely dialectical, in which a crypto-missionary will to power may still be operating, from the truly dialogical dialogue, in which each partner remains open to the possibility of being converted by the other.

5. In the modern world the secular has become sacred. Recently awakened ecological and environmental sensitivity in many forms, along with 'religious' concern for peace, justice, food, health, and so on, attests to this transition. Modern Man's painful discovery of no longer being rulers of the universe but its responsible partners or stewards is a basic religious experience. Human religiousness cannot henceforward dissociate itself from this earth—the proper *oikos* of any ecumenism, the habit of the human family—and every effort toward salvation now calls for a genuine integration with the entire universe. Geology is also theology, or in my old expression, theophysics also belongs to physics. Ecumenical ecumenism has neither a closed agenda nor a closed membership. Any way of life has a right to a seat at the roundtable of the *ecumene.*

6. Ecumenical ecumenism also keeps an open seat for those attitudes that we may call totalitarian. Their desire to dominate the whole scene does not warrant their exclusion. The ecumenical attitude is ready to reexamine again and again the rules of the encounter, although it cannot agree that anybody should dictate such rules. Sometimes dialogue may not be possible, but it should never be closed a priori. One has even to reckon with the possibility that the totalitarian view may be right, even if at a given stage of the dialogue one cannot agree with it. Representatives of the christian tradition should bear the burden and share the experience of such a totalitarian attitude, which has often been theirs—edifying and numerous exceptions notwithstanding. Ecumenism does not exclude the risk of some of the partners' having a hidden agenda. It will denounce it; if discovered, bring it to light; and respond according to the new data. But it will never foreclose communication.

7. Just like all the previous encounters and clashes of religions, the widened ecumenical dialogue I am proposing does not take place in a vacuum. The bitter lessons of crusades, holy wars, colonialisms, imperialisms, and domination of all types should warn us against using religion or religious language to justify unconfessed or unclarified impulses. The ecumenical discourse is, of course, not exclusively political or economic,

but it takes place within a context of politico-economic power relationships that cannot be abstracted from the dialogue. Religion is not an independent variable, though not simply reducible to other factors. Ecumenism is never totally neutral, and it has to take into account this intrinsic limitation. We do not discuss disincarnated doctrines. We are all situated in time and space and in a world of socio-politico-economic factors that condition not only our views and expressions but also our very relationship with one another. We should not ignore those factors, putting them into brackets as if they were irrelevant, but bring them to our consciousness is much as possible—with the aid of the other's sometimes pitiless and even, according to us, unjust criticism.

8. Ecumenism is not unqualified irenism. It does not prevent struggle and disagreement but provides a platform for it, insofar as it succeeds in establishing a dialogue. Ecumenism will sometimes have to wait with the hope that what appears impossible at a certain moment may become plausible at another. The history of religious encounters offers us many such examples. But it will refrain from organizing a crusade against atheists or so-called 'unbelievers', for example. Yet dialogue does not exclude controversy; encounter does not mean agreement. Ecumenism does not aim directly at unity but at understanding; it does not dream of uniformity but the closest possible harmony. The power of evil is not disregarded, but the very ways to overcome it form part of the ecumenical endeavor.

9. No ecumenical dialogue can be monolingual. To assume that in and through a single human language we can understand the universal human experience is perhaps the last, even if unconscious, remnant of intellectual imperialism, and to trust in translations is philosophical naiveté. True ecumenical ecumenism is a two-way traffic. The dialogue has to take place in the languages of at least two of the traditions—not only as mere means of communication but, more important, as representing two basic human attitudes. Otherwise, the dialogue has already taken place in the mind and heart of the translator. This minimal requirement of bilingualism is essential to any ecumenical enterprise. We cannot understand if we do not bring the case to our own categories, but then we already see the case according to our familiar patterns. This is equally valid for our partner. It is not sufficient, say, to formulate hindu tenets and find their christian equivalents, even if the two parties would still disagree. One has equally to attempt to bring the christian tenets into hindu equivalents. In other words, it is not only that we should strive for hindu

answers to christian questions; we should equally try to give christian answers to hindu questions. It is a multivoiced dialogue. Not only are the many answers accepted, but also the many questions are entertained.

10. Any impulse toward ecumenism can be viable only if it recognizes an un-understandable ground of understanding. This un-understandable point, be it transcendent or immanent, is all that prevents us from being closed-in inside our own self-understanding. Were we not mutually to accept such a *mysterium* that both surpasses and sustains our understanding, then, obviously, if I am right, you are wrong, and we have no higher controlling understanding of our respective positions. This does not exclude, as already said, the fanatic and totalitarian partner as long as the partner accepts a minimum basis for communication— although with these people alone no ecumenism would be possible. Ecumenism has the power of its precariousness. It is based on prayer.

Simply stated, ecumenical ecumenism implies the rediscovery of a basic and enduring task of religion: to contribute to the freeing of a full humanness for humanity. At this point, perhaps, we should hearken to the last words of the Buddha: "Work out your salvation with diligence" and connect them with what he had said before: "Be lamps unto one another."

8

Intrareligious Dialogue according to Ramon Llull

THE DIALOGUE IN THE *LIBRE DEL GENTIL E LOS TRES SAVIS* takes place in a land which jews, christians and muslims each considered their own. Ramon Llull speaks to us of the concord needed between the three most important western powers. If we had listened to him, history would have been different. But perhaps we can still take heed today. . . .

* * * * *

Leaving to one side the powerful aesthetic force of the "beautiful maiden" riding on her "handsome palfrey" and the symbolism of the five trees and the 217 flowers, I shall restrict myself to commenting on his prophetic and ecumenical vision so full of lessons for our own time.

I would like *first of all* to mention his boldness in heaping praise not only on the pagan, who is referred to as a wise man and considered good,

111

but also on the jew and the saracen. They may not have the truth, but Llull has not a moment's doubt that they have goodness, and the Mallorcan philosopher constantly repeats that you cannot have one without the other. One of his basic arguments in fact consists in the ontological correlation between "right and greatness," "wisdom and love," "love and perfection." This is not, therefore, a fight between enemies. The idea is not to beat an opponent but to convince a companion. Each of them greets the others "in his language and according to his customs." This is more than tolerance. Ramon is telling us that all religions are good because they produce good men and wise. The time is the end of the thirteenth century, after two centuries of crusades! And Llull is daring enough not to condemn anyone—what's more, not to make anyone win! The pagan converts to God but puts off his entry into one of the three great religions. What matters is to come out of oneself (love) and worship God—that is, to enter into the Mystery and take part.

Second, the book shows that disagreement among men is a leading evil that must be eradicated, and this is the first task for religion. This lack of brotherhood is a religious crime and not just a political fact. Ramon is well aware that the official religions have for too long ignored harmony between men, when not in fact themselves promoting religious wars and fights.

This is the great scandal of institutionalized religion! The pagan's "woes and torments" echo those of Ramon: "In despair and lamenting was Ramon under a fine tree and he sang his despair to ease his pain." Thus begins his voluminous *Arbre de Ciència.*

We must seek religious harmony among people not through crusades and inquisitions, but through mutual respect and joint research and, especially, through dialogue. Llull conveys his conviction that men are subjected to a power that is higher than all of us, which in his writing is not the monotheistic God but Lady Intelligence: the power to *intuslegere* the nature of reality.

Third, the rules of the game laid down by Llull for a dialogue between cultures are prophetically valid for our present moment.

1. Debate must never be mere intellectual curiosity and certainly not academic competition but must arise from an existential yearning; it must spring from the experience of human hardship, from seeing the disastrous results of disunion, and from a realization of its betrayal of history and of the very essence of religion. This is not a luxury! The tears, laments, prayers, and prostrations of our text are not just literary flourishes.

2. The dialogue has to take place on neutral ground, outside the city, in a conducive setting and a pleasant atmosphere: a nice orchard with its wholesome, sweet-smelling fruits. Above all, it must not be carried out in a situation of inequality, with one side owning all the dollars and all the political power, dominating the situation or imposing its language. Religious dialogue is not possible when some ride well shod and others walk barefoot. Geographical serenity is a symbol of historical equanimity. Man is a geological as well as a historical being.

3. The conversation must not only keep to a civil vein; it must also be directed by an impartial but not indifferent third party. The pagan will be the arbiter, and the others will not interrupt each other but will speak in rigorous chronological order and will apologize to one other before and afterward. The act of contrition must be the "introit" for any interreligious dialogue.

4. Arguments of authority—which today we would call arguments of force—must not be used. Paradoxically, quotations from the Holy Scriptures are not suited to interreligious discourse. We should not take our own premises as a basis for the others. Neither "*Gott mit uns*" nor "In [our] God we trust" are postulates for interreligious dialogue. It is in the name of God that some of the greatest crimes on earth have been committed. Dialogue does not presuppose a particular belief, so much as simply faith in the very act of the encounter—which therefore becomes a religious act.

5. They do not conceal their opinions, and the three wise men do not hesitate to show up "false opinions and errors." The three monotheists make no bones about their belief that the others are on the wrong track. But in spite of this, they talk and look for agreement. Each one must be true to his own conscience. Interreligious discourse is not like diplomatic negotiation.

6. The discussion is not a closed dialogue but goes under the judgment of one who does not even "have knowledge of God" or believe "in resurrection" at the risk that this stranger might even be shocked at the small-mindedness of the established religions. The boldness of this approach is unknown even in our day. Let me emphasize that christians and muslims, catholics or atheists, or whoever will never begin a fruitful dialogue if they just discuss things among themselves—that is, if they don't make a joint effort as reflected in the dialogue of the three wise men

and the pagan. Take, for example, the issue of peace in our day. Religion is not an end in itself so much as a means.

7. The effort of religious understanding is constitutively unfinished, in-finite; it will continue as long as necessary because it is in itself the manifestation of our contingency. Perhaps this is the most important and most revealing trait. The dialogue takes place without foreseeable results and independent of human will. No one knows what the outcome of the encounter will be: No one knows which side the pagan will come down on. The unity of truth to which the human heart aspires is not uniformity of opinions but perhaps their equivalence, complementarity, or even polarity. Everything suggests that the pagan has found a primordial religiousness that makes him break out with the speech that so strikes "the three wise men" and that all three of them can approve without betraying their respective confessions. This speech speaks of the three theological virtues, the four cardinal virtues, and the seven vices and virtues, so as to "wake the sleeping greats," he says with clear (hidden) intentions at the end of the book.

All these traits can be summarized in one: the passage from interreligious dialogue to intrareligious dialogue; from exteriority to interiority, from the condemnation of others to the examination of one's own conscience, from the problem of political power to personal issues, from dogma to mysticism, if you prefer. Until humanity's religious problem is seen and understood as an intimate, personal problem, until religion is fathomed and discovered as a dimension of the human being—and therefore something affecting all of us, until there is despair and lamenting over the human destiny we all form part of, until then we shall not be able to distinguish doctrinal disputes, political rivalries, and personal ambition from the true religious act that is the common search for Man's very purpose and cooperation and accomplishment of the very destiny of the universe. Religion is far more a constitutive dimension of humans than an institution.

But let's get back to the *Libre del gentil e los tres savis*. As the reader is free to enjoy the text for himself, I shall simply retell what I think is one of the most important elements in the myth implicit in the book:

> . . . As the infidels had long taken part . . . as we, contemporaries of this declining twentieth century, have already been well-acquainted with modern civilization for some centuries and, despite the unquestionable advantages for us (not for everyone), "having understood their false opinions and errors," and being witnesses to the deterioration in human

life and the results ensuing from the violation of nature, the acceleration
of the rhythms of the cosmos, the monetization of culture, the quantifi-
cation of existence; realizing, also, that we have now lost even "the
words by which is best expressed" the current situation, we want to
speak of a pagan—that is, of the people who make up at least eighty per-
cent of the human population—and of her dialogue with the three wise
men. . . .

Not by "God's ordainment," but by a particular dynamics of human
history, "it happened" that on our planet there are people who weep and
search without hope and without consolation. When there isn't famine,
exploitation, dictatorship, torture, and war in one place, there are drugs,
depression, debauchery, and distress in another. These people, also, met
up with the three wise men . . . . One knew all there was to know about
Science. His forebears were Hebrews and Egyptians. The other said he
possessed *Sentiment.* His ancestors separated from the first wise men
twenty centuries ago so as to put love above all else, in the belief that God
was love. The third wise man was *Will.* His origins came from the ineffec-
tiveness of the first two when it came to putting things into practice. These
three wise men have been trying to put the world to rights since ancient
times.

But the pagan, the people, the man in the street, has lived—lives—
joylessly, in spite of the great discoveries of Science, Sentiment, and Will,
or perhaps he has just lost hope in these supposed panaceas.

The three wise men held very beautiful dialogues, and the "mass
media" of the privileged were responsible for spreading their point of
view with a barrage of ideologies of all sorts. They called this education,
information, and even religion: "Science will save the world. Nothing can
be done without Love. Ideas are useless unless they are Realized."

Our "pagan," who listened attentively to them, was nevertheless left
perplexed. "Must we wait for the last discovery before we can be happy?
Isn't love very often counterproductive? Doesn't pure praxis often lead to
destruction and fanaticism?"

In this story we have avoided grand discussions among Science, Sentiment, and Will. The whole of the history of humanity is contained in it.
But neither Peace nor Concord seem to arise from it. Perhaps later understanding will be reached and the problems of the world will be solved, but
while the uproar, competition, and consumption continue, how many
more generations will have to be sacrificed? Must we continue waiting for
the future or has the time already come for us to transcend history?

The pagan—that is, the people of three-quarters of the world, no longer believe in either Science, Religion, or Politics, and perhaps it is time to listen to them in their pilgrimage through the forests of this world.

The people went, then, to "the great forest," but they did not take pleasure in "the shores and springs and meadows and the many different kinds of birds in the trees that sang so sweetly . . . ," because almost everything was contaminated and only the rich could visit the most distant and "natural" spots. The palfrey on which the damsel Intelligence used to ride had died of starvation and from the stench of petrol, and the Lady was not to be seen anywhere.

But lo and behold, our pagan, our people—so to speak, after much walking, suffering, and brooding, one day saw a damsel arrive on foot. She was middle-aged and was not "nobly dressed," but she was "of agreeable countenance."

"What is your name?" they asked the damsel finally.

"My name is *Grace*," she answered.

"And what does that mean?" they asked her.

"That means that I am agreeable, filled with gratitude, graceful, gratifying, and gratuitous. I do everything 'gratis' because I like what I do, I am grateful for everything because no one owes me anything, I find everything gratifying because I ask for nothing; they say I behave gracefully because I do not do things for any extrinsic reason, and that is why people find me agreeable, congratulate me, and are grateful because I admit no form of payment; in that way, no one can be ungrateful to me or fall into disgrace before me."

"And what did the people understand?" I asked intrigued.

"Personally," said a confidant, "I understood that life is worth living in itself, that worrying over the means distracts us from the ends, that the object is joy, and that this joy surprises us when we know how to live the tempiternal moments (which are not outside time but are not stifled by it, either). Together we understood, also, that if our life is not freed from the exclusive weight of history, if our ideals do not overcome those of self-absorbed men enclosed in prisons they call cities, if our loves do not transcend the crust of things, we are not really living. We also understood that if we want to reduce everything to quantitative parameters, to the measure of reason, and to a fleeting time through which we pass unnoticed, we shall not grasp the mystery of existence, the beauty of things, the truth of reality, and therefore we shall never achieve that well-being that surpasses all conception, the God that was the symbol of Mystery and who now perhaps takes on other Names. The solution for the world and for ourselves does not lie in the models of the Abrahamic traditions. The pagan was not convinced. Perhaps the solution does not lie anywhere because it isn't static.

"But," the people said, "we have not yet managed to grasp this Grace business. We heard her arriving, we felt her touch, and we were grateful. We saw once more that the world was beautiful, that everything is gratuitous, if we share it graciously. That's why this Joy, which is another name for Grace, does not paralyze our action, but strengthens us in our delight for justice. . . ."

9

Śūnyatā and Plêrôma

The Buddhist and Christian Response

to the Human Predicament

ἐκ τοῦ πληρώματος αὐτοῦ
ἡμεις πάντες ἐλάβομεν.
From his fullness we have all received.
　　　—Jn. I:16

pratītyasamutpādaḥ śunyatām
[the] interdependence [of all things is] emptiness
　　　—Nāgārjuna, *Mūlamadhyamaka-kārikā*, XXIV, 18

1. THE HUMAN PREDICAMENT

IN SPITE OF THE SCORES OF ATTEMPTS AT DEFINING RELIGION, I may venture this simple and brief statement: Religion is the path we follow in order to reach the purpose of life, or, shorter, religion is the *way of salvation*. One has to add immediately that here the words 'way' and 'salvation' do not claim any specific content; rather they stand for the existential pilgrimage we undertake in the belief that this enterprise will help us achieve the final purpose or end of life.[1] A *way to fulfillment*—if we prefer.

In other words, under the particular perspective that we may call religion, every human culture presents three elements: (1) a vision of Man as she actually appears to be *(hic et nunc)*, (2) a certain more or less developed notion of the end or final station of each *(illic et postea)*, and (3) the means for going from the former situation to the latter.[2]

The first element may be called the *human predicament*, that is, the particular view of how Man is seen and evaluated. I use this expression rather than the more common 'human condition' in order to stress that not all religions view Man's factual situation along the lines 'condition' suggests. Man is not independent of what we take ourselves to be, and the human condition is precisely conditioned by Man's own view of it. By human predicament I mean the factual status of Man as it is evaluated in a particular conception forming part of that factual status itself.

No religion, and much less those we shall consider, can be encompassed in a monolithic doctrine, as if a single doctrine could sum up all it stands for. This chapter will choose only a pair of notions, one from each tradition, to represent an orthodox view in the respective religions.

The human predicament seen by the buddhist tradition could be summarized: (1) in a philosophical presupposition, the anātmavāda;[3] (2) in a theological statement, the *āryasatyāni*,[4] which expands the anthropocosmic intuition of *sarva duḥkha*;[5] and (3) in a moral injunction best rendered by the last words of the Buddha: "Work out your salvation with diligence."[6]

The human predicament seen by the christian tradition could be summarized: (1) in a philosophical presupposition, the creation of the world;[7] (2) in a theological statement, the redeeming or saving power of Christ,[8] which expands the cosmotheandric intuition of the incarnation;[9] and (3) in a moral injunction best rendered by the words of Christ summing up the Law and the Prophets: "You shall love the Lord your God with all your heart, and all your soul, and all your might. . . .[10] You shall love your neighbor as yourself."[11]

We may try to express in our own words the gist of this double vision. It should be remembered that until recently these two traditions agreed about the human predicament. Right or wrong, they seem to concur in saying that we are endowed with a craving—literally a thirst[12]—or with a lust—literally a desire[13]—that is the cause of our unhappiness. The two religions will elaborate this as an Ignorance or a

Fall so that enlightenment or redemption is required to overcome the human predicament. In any case the human predicament is neither as it should be nor as it could be. The Buddha[14] and the Christ[15] claim to remedy this situation. A human being has to transcend Man's present condition in order to be freed, that is, disentangled from the wheel of *saṁsāra*,[16] from this *kosmos*.[17] Both buddhism and christianity stand for human liberation.[18]

Here both traditions express an almost universal human experience. Both are convinced that Man is a being not yet finished, a reality unachieved, growing, becoming, on the way, a pilgrim. This is the human predicament. The real problem lies in the response that each of these two world religions gives to it.

2. THE BUDDHIST AND CHRISTIAN RESPONSES

a. Nirvāṇa and Sôtêría

As we have said, the second element of all religions is the notion that there is an end or a final station of Man. We, these unfinished beings, are not to remain as we are but have to undergo a more or less radical transformation, a change, in order to reach that state that buddhism calls *nirvāṇa*[19] and christianity *sôtêría*.[20] Religion is the dynamism toward a *terminus ad quem*, originating in a disconformity with the *status quo*.

Significantly enough, the canonical writings of both traditions do not seem inclined to limit the nature of these two terms. *Nirvāṇa* is simply the cessation of becoming,[21] of all *saṁskāra*,[22] of all links,[23] of every thirst.[24] It is the blowing out of all the *karma*,[25] the indescribable term of which not even being can be predicated,[26] the radical originating power of everything,[27] and the end with neither way in nor out.[28] It is beyond all dialectic[29] and thinking,[30] without subject or object.[31] The whole effort lies in reaching it, not in describing or understanding it.[32] But this sentence is false if it is taken to link *nirvāṇa* in any way with our will or imagination.[33] *Nirvāṇa* is "unborn, unbecome, unmade, unaggregated."[34] *Nirvāṇa* is not transcendent in the usual sense of the word; were it to transcend anything, it would already be transcendentally linked with what it transcends.[35] *Nirvāṇa* is the mere destruction or rather the unmaking[36] of all that is and that, by the very fact that it can be undone, destroyed, and negated, proves its nonreality so that *nirvāṇa* is the most positive 'thing' because it destroys nothingness.

The same vagueness seems to mark the christian scriptural idea of *sôtêría*. It is salvation from perdition,[37] from death,[38] through Christ,[39] who leads to salvation.[40] It seems to be eternal[41] for it is the salvation of our lives.[42] Often salvation is used without further qualification, in apparent acceptance of common usage.[43] There is a way,[44] a word,[45] and a knowledge[46] of salvation. Jesus is the savior;[47] he saves the people from their sins,[48] and there is salvation in no one else.[49]

In other words, neither *nirvāṇa* nor *sôtêría* has developed cosmological or metaphysical underpinnings. *Nirvāṇa* or rather *parinirvāṇa* is the extinction of the human condition and *sôtêría* the freeing from sin.

b. Śūnyatā and Plêrôma

It would require an entire volume to render even cursorily the different interpretations of these central notions. As already indicated, we shall alleviate the difficulty by choosing two significant examples and offering only the bare sketch of their doctrines. The two key words here are *śūnyatā*[50] and *plêrôma*, [51] emptiness and fullness. Both are radical and both could be said to represent most emphatically the quintessence of their respective traditions. Furthermore, as the prima facie meaning of the words themselves suggests, both terms seem to be at total variance, not only with one another, but also with modern humanistic traditions.

The end of the journey, the goal of Man is by definition *nirvāṇa* or *sôtêría*, but the nature of this goal is supposed to be *śūnyatā* in the former case and *plêrôma* in the latter, according to some schools in the respective traditions.

In complete harmony with the central Buddhist intuition of *nairātmyavāda*, or the doctrine of the ultimate unsubstantiality of all things, the concept of *śūnyatā* (vacuity, voidness, emptiness) tries to express the very essence of the absolute, the ultimate nature or reality of all things.[52]

Śūnyavāda is not philosophical nihilism or metaphysical agnosticism, but a positive and concrete affirmation, one of the deepest human intuitions regarding the ultimate structure of reality.[53] It says that everything, absolutely everything, that falls under the range of our experience— actual or possible—is void of that (superimposed and thus only falsely appearing) consistency with which we tend to embellish our contingency.

All, including the faculty of reason with which we express this very idea, is in the grip of contingent flux. The 'other shore' in the recurring Buddhist metaphor is so totally transcendent that it does not exist; the very thought of it mystifies and negates it.[54] 'Nirvāṇa is saṁsāra and saṁsāra is nirvāṇa,' says one well-known formulation,[55] repeated again and again in different forms.[56] There is no way to go to the other shore because there is no bridge, nor even another shore. This recognition is the highest wisdom, the advaitic or nondualistic intuition or the prajñāpāramitā. To recognize saṁsāra as saṁsāra, that is, as the flux of existence and that same existence as being in flux, is already the beginning of enlightenment, not because one transcends it (for there is no 'other place' behind or beyond) but because this very recognition sweeps away the veil of ignorance that consists precisely in taking as real or substantial that which is only pure void and vacuity.[57] That is why only silence is the right attitude—not because the question has no answer, but because we realize the non-sense of the question itself, because there can be no questioning of the unquestionable (it would be a contradiction) and there can be no answer when there is no question.[58] Who can question the unquestionable? Certainly not the unquestionable itself, and from this questionable world there can be no question about what cannot be questioned. Anything that can be questioned is certainly not unquestionable. Thus the ontic silence of the Buddha.

In complete harmony with the central christian doctrine of the Incarnation, the concept of plêrôma (fullness, fulfillment) expresses the end of Man and of all creation.[59] Not only did the Redeemer come at the fullness of time,[60] but he let all those who believe in him be filled with his own fullness,[61] for of his fullness we have all received,[62] and in him the fullness of the deity dwells bodily.[63] It is then the fullness of God[64] that fills everything, though there is a distention, a period of expectation and hope until the restoration of all things.[65] Once the whole world is subjected unto him to whom all has been subjected, then he will subject himself fully to God so that God will be all in all.[66]

Apart from the possible hermetic, gnostic and other uses of the word plêrôma, christian tradition has understood this message to mean being called to be as perfect as the heavenly Father;[67] being one with Christ[68] as he is one with his Father,[69] and thus becoming not like God, as the Tempter offered,[70] but God itself[71] through our union with the Son by the work and grace of the Spirit.[72]

Theôsis, divinization, was the technical word used during long centuries of christian tradition, and the simplest formula was to say that God has become Man in order that Man might become God.[73]

The entire christian economy is the transformation of the cosmos until the new heaven and the new earth,[74] which includes the resurrection of the flesh.[75] Our destiny is to become God, to reach the other shore where divinity dwells by means of the transformation that requires a new birth in order to enter the kingdom of heaven.[76] *Metanoia,* change of heart, of life, and ultimately a passage from death to new life, was the central topic of Christ's proclamation,[77] for which John the Baptist, the forerunner, had already prepared the way.[78]

We should try now to understand what these words symbolize within their respective traditions.

Without *śūnyatā* thought is bound.[79] The fact is neither that the bound one is released nor the unbound one unreleased.[80] To realize the emptiness of all things is the culmination of all wisdom *(prajñā),* which leads to the discovery of the radical relativity of all things and their interdependence *(pratītyasamutpāda),* which begins the realization of *nirvāṇa.* In point of fact there is more a sense of equality than of hierarchy among these four notions.[81] We are not describing four steps, epistemological or ontological, but four ways of conveying one and the same realization: the realization that there is no-thing definitive in this world and that any other possibility, even the thought of it, is still linked with our 'this-worldly' experience and hence conditioned, dependent, not definitive—in a word, empty. Were it not for this emptiness things could not move; change would be impossible because material bodies could not move if there were no space between them. Emptiness is the very condition for the type of existence proper to things, and there is no-thing else, for any-thing else that could be would be affected by the same emptiness, by the very fact that we consider it possible and thus an object of our thought.

> There neither water nor earth,
> neither fire nor air can subsist,
> there the stars do not shine nor the sun illumine,
> there the moon does not brighten nor darkness exist.[82]

Without *plêrôma* there would be no place for God, and human existence would make no sense. Man is more than Man; when he wants to be merely Man he degenerates into a beast.[83] He is destined for higher things.[84] Whenever he is disquiet,[85] whenever he searches for something, it is because God is already calling him.[86] Divine transcendence is safeguarded because christian divinization is, properly speaking, more a 'filiation' than an undiscriminated fusion with the Father. The christian Trinity is here the warranty for the appropriate distinction without separation. Man, and with him the entire universe, becomes one with the Son by the power and grace of the Spirit; as the Son a person is one with the

Father but never becomes the Father. Even more, orthodox christian thinking will stress in one way or another that while the Son *is* God of God, Light of Light, Man *becomes* one with the Son and so reaches the Godhead in and through the Son. Man's temporality ever remains a scar, as it were, in the very heart of his being. Divinization, christian tradition will stress, does not mean human alienation precisely because we are of divine nature.[87] We are called upon to share God in a fuller way, to go home to our primordial nature and origin. Divinization reestablishes the image that had been distorted and makes us what we are really called upon to become. Divine sonship is the truly human vocation. What Christ is by nature[88] is what Christ as our brother[89] has enabled us to be and do by adoption (redemption): to share his sonship[90] in a new birth,[91] born again of water and the Spirit.[92]

3. RELIGIONS AND THE HUMANIZING OF MAN

It was a Greek who said that Man is the measure of all things.[95] But it was another Greek who refuted him[94] and further affirmed it is God and not Man who is the measure of all things,[95] so that his disciple could say that Man, though mortal, should not satisfy himself with mortal things, but strive to become immortal.[96] They all might have remembered one of their ancestors saying: 'The idiosyncrasy of Man is his *daimôn.'*[97]

It was from hebrew inspiration that it is written God created Man in his own image and likeness[98] and again from the same source that the sentence was often reversed and considered more a definition of God than a description of Adam: God in the image of Adam.[99]

It was a jew influenced by greek culture and by what his faith regarded as a unique event who wrote that it was the divine Word dwelling with God that became flesh,[100] and a Roman who presented this same person as the Man.[101]

It was a kṣatriya from the East who refused to speak about God and declined to indulge in merely theoretical speculations.[102] This same man was directly and exclusively concerned with giving concrete and effective advice about handling the human predicament.[103] Reacting against the religious inflation of his time and against the deleterious human condition of his contemporaries, he centered all his life on showing how to be rid of the almost all-pervading human disquiet and anxiety, refusing even to undergird his teachings with any anthropology.[104] In this, he echoes the tradition of his own culture that had so strongly emphasized that:

> The Man, indeed, is the All,
> What has been and what is to be,[105]

because the primordial Man is the supreme reality.[106] No wonder buddhism was to flourish in the humanistic soil par excellence, the Confucian
world, and in chinese culture at large.[107]

Following up the functional description of religion we have already
given, we may yet add that religion is the way in which Man handles his
human predicament in order to steer it toward a somewhat better situation. Today we are acutely aware of the urgency and difficulty of performing such a task. Here the sketch of two great religious traditions
could prove of some value. With this we are saying that Comparative Religion, far from being merely a comparison of religions or a historical discipline, is in fact a study of ultimate human problems—that is, of religious
situations—with the aid of more than one religious tradition, so that by
illuminating the concrete human predicament with the accumulated
experience of humankind we may be in a better position to understand it.

a. Buddhism, Christianity, and Humanism

In this light we may now focus on the contemporary humanistic situation.
For some decades humanism has been a powerful word.[108] It expresses a
valuable myth that in the traditionally christian countries can be understood as a reaction against a certain devaluation of the human in favor of
something supernatural.[109] The twentieth century has seen the birth of all
possible humanisms: atheistic, scientific, new, classical, modern,
medieval, social, and even hyperbolical. Isolated voices have even been
raised in favor of hindu and buddhist humanisms. It is difficult to deci-
pher what is not a humanism, except some exaggerated and obviously
inhuman tendencies in several ideologies. We are weary of certain dehumanizing trends in established religions. Humanism may be a healthy
reaction. Currently, modern ideologies and so-called technocracies of
every sort are also seen as dehumanizing forces. Not only are a transcendent heaven and an eternal hell now viewed as dehumanizing, but society, techniques, modern cities, and so forth are also seen as deleterious to
us. It is in this context that some would challenge traditional religions to
really serve in this task of humanizing Man. Here we may add some
reflections from the buddhist and christian viewpoint.

To begin with, religions are very sensitive about being dictated to
from the outside or being told to serve anything, for they suppose them-

selves to be above any servitude. What matters is not 'saving' the human predicament according to our individual opinions, they will say, but seeing the situation as it really is in the light of the religious tradition. Perhaps what is called the 'Humanizing of Man' is nothing but his entanglement and damnation.

Avoiding these touchy attitudes, which come only from superficial approaches, we would like to approach the problem from the perspective of Comparative Religion or Philosophy of Religion as we defined it above.

The roughly seven thousand years of historical memory show a common pattern present almost everywhere: the human desire for immortality. Overcoming death has always been a central religious and human concern. As to the means, religions differ. From the point of view of History of Religions one could be inclined to interpret the thrust toward divinization as a means for rescuing human beings from the clutches of death as well as from the fear of nature or from the grip of the whole cosmos. In almost every religious tradition, the fundamental trait of divinization is immortality. The human predicament is that mortal Man must overcome his situation in the different ways offered by the most diverse religions. One way or another, traditional religions want to overcome the human condition by reaching the unconditioned. Divinization could appear phenomenologically as the unconditioning of the human condition. We reach the divine (which may be variously interpreted) once we have overcome our mortal condition. Christianity would be a peculiar instance of this attitude. Its doctrine of the Trinity lets it defend a total divinization (union with the Son) without destroying the "God-Man" difference.

Buddhism offers a different attitude. It does not want to uncondition but rather to decondition human beings; it is not concerned with reaching transcendence but with overcoming immanence; it does not care as much about God as about deconditioning us in a radical and ultimate way. We have to cease being what we *are,* not in order to become another thing, not even God, but in order to negate totally the human and worldly situation. Buddhism shatters the human dream of any imaginable or thinkable survival.

Over against these two, present-day secularity could represent a new attitude that considers time, that is, the temporal universe, to be real and positive, and so not to be transcended.[110] Secularity does not mean unconditioning or deconditioning the human predicament, but soberly recognizing it as it appears. There is no escaping it or denying it. The driving force behind any humanism is to make us really ourselves and nothing but ourselves, and we, humanism would say, should banish any fear of worldly or superworldly powers. We have come of age; we need not fear being ourselves. But having overcome our fear of nature, of God and the Gods, we now begin to fear ourselves and our societal reality. So the entire problem crops up all over again. We might ask, what are we that we have to be made ourselves? Who is this being who needs to be made, to become what he is not—(yet ?).

b. Homo Viator

An in-depth study of these three answers may perhaps furnish humanity with a more elaborated model than any of the one-sided solutions so far proposed.[111] This would be a task of Comparative Religion.[112]

We may observe a double assumption: (1) Man is an unachieved being; (2) this achievement is the real Man.

The first part is almost a matter of course. The human status quo is never definitive. There is always room for change, repentance, hope, enlightenment, salvation, betterment, and the like. The human predicament is infinite because it is not finite, not finished. Man is an open being; we 'ek-sist' by stretching out our being, along time and space at least.

The second assumption is less apparent and yet equally common to the three fundamental attitudes under analysis. No human tradition, religious or secular, endorses our alienation. To convert us radically into an altogether different being would not only be heterodox and foreign to any tradition but nonsensical too. Any difference has meaning only within and over against an underlying identity. An absolute change is a contradiction in terms, for nothing would remain of what is supposed to have changed.

If Buddhism wants to annihilate us, to decondition our human condition, to extinguish in us all *saṁsāric* existence, all remnants of creatureliness, it is because it presupposes that Man *is* not, that there is no *ātman*, so that the blowing out *(nirvāṇa)* of all spatio-temporal and experiential structures is then the 'true realization of our authentic "nature"'. The destruction of all our constructions is the real human liberation, and yet this does not conflict with the central orthodox buddhist attitude of universal compassion *(karuṇā)*,[113] unlimited friendliness. You can embody a serene, joyful, and even pragmatically effective loving attitude only if you have realized the *śūnyatā* of all things.

If christianity wants to divinize us, to let us share the divine nature and return through Christ to the Father, it is because it presupposes that the divine nature is the ultimate and most intimate constitution of a human being.[114] We are an offspring of God[115] and have to go back to the Father to realize fully what we are.[116] Yet this does not conflict with the distinction between God and us, nor with the christian emphasis on death and resurrection, new birth and total repentance. The risen Christ, like the risen christian, is certainly a new creature[117] but not another one *(aliud non alius)*. The person is the same.[118] In scholastic terms: *gratia non destruit, sed-supponit et perficit naturam.*[119] God does not become God, yet Man becomes what Man is not yet.

Similarly, if humanism wants to humanize us by making us recognize and accept our human condition, and to help us resist the temptation of escaping into realms of unreality, it is because it presupposes that the future of Man *is* Man and that our authentic dignity consists in affirming our humanness in spite of every allurement from above and below. We have to face our future with daring and dignity, and even when confronted with the absurd or the meaningless, we must accept and affirm ourselves.[120] This attitude does not contravene the humanistic dogma that denies any substantial instance superior to us, for the secularized 'future' plays many of the roles of the monotheistic God; but humanism also requires a proper belief in humanity, which is a belief in the unseen. Humanism demands of us as heroic a posture as any traditional religion.

Nevertheless, despite all the structural similarities between these worldviews, we cannot overlook their differing anthropologies, that is, the different conceptions of Man and ultimately of reality underlying them. Nothing is more barren and dangerous than superficial agreements and merely tactical compromises. The injunction to humanize Man, which practically everyone would admit, means various and opposite things to different worldviews and religious traditions. The real encounter comes when we cease to analyze structural patterns and concentrate on the nature of the purpose itself. What is humanizing? We can do no more here than ask the question.

c. The Crossing of the Ways

If the study of religion means anything today, it has to address itself to this problem. A whole new *methodic* is required because we can no longer pose the problem in the limited and particularized way we have done until now, leaving the world cut into cultural compartments. Even modern humanism is, by and large, as provincial and limited to its own peculiar conception of "Man" and Reality as many of the more traditional cultures it criticizes. Nobody can decide a priori what it means to humanize our being, nor can this totally depend on a single anthropology. It requires not a methodology but a *methodic* of its own, which makes its way in and through the mutual interaction and possible cross-fertilization of different religions and cultures. A dialogical dialogue is necessary here. This dialogical dialogue, which differs from a dialectical one, stands on the assumption that nobody has access to the universal horizon of human experience and that only by not postulating the rules of the encounter from a single side can we proceed toward a deeper and more universal understanding of ourselves and thus come closer to our own realization. At this point, to want to humanize humanity according to some preconceived scheme, even if convincing for some, would amount to repeating the same mistake so many religious traditions have made in the conviction that they possessed the truth or had the duty, and so the right, to proclaim their message of salvation. No one can be excluded from the task of humanizing us; no human tradition should be silent in this common task.

We may add a final thought, the distinction between eclecticism and syncretism. The former is an uncritical mixture of religious traditions and an agreement among them obtained by chopping off all possible discrepancies in favor of an amorphous common denominator. Syncretism is allowing for a possible assimilation of elements by virtue of which these elements cease to be foreign bodies so that organic growth within each tradition is possible, and the mutual fecundation of religious traditions becomes a genuine option.[121]

Avoiding eclecticisms, but having in mind possible interactions—although we should not minimize the existing tensions, philosophical, theological, or religious, between the traditions under consideration—we may envision corrections, warnings and complementarities that may not only allay mutual suspicions and so often one-sided positions, but also help cultivate a real human growth and thus contribute positively to a concrete humanization of human life on earth.

Let me indicate a few points for study. The central buddhist concern is a timely reminder both to christianity and to every sort of humanism that no amount of 'revelation' or 'reason' justifies manipulating humans under the guise of 'the will of God' or the 'demands of Reason' in order to steer humanity and the world to clearly defined goals. The ultimate goal is always so ineffable that it does not even exist. Buddhism is the thorough defense of the ultimate, absolutely ungraspable, mystery of existence. The mystery here is immanent.

The central christian concern is a timely reminder to buddhism and to all the humanisms that no amount of self-effort and goodwill suffices to handle the human predicament adequately; we must remain constantly open to unexpected and unforeseeable eruptions of Reality itself, which christians may want to call God or divine Providence. Christianity stands for the unselfish and authentic defense of the primordial rights of Reality, of which we are not the masters. The mystery here is transcendent.

Humanism, further, is a timely reminder to buddhism and christianity not only that traditional religions have often forgotten their own sayings—like the nonauthority of the Buddha,[122] who may even become the greatest obstacle to realizing one's own Buddha nature,[123] or like the Sabbath made for us and not vice versa,[124] and the freedom of the children of God,[125] made free by truth itself[126]—but also that the humanizing of "Man" cannot lose sight of the concrete person to be humanized. Pointing out the way or proclaiming the message will never suffice if the conditions are not given and worked for. Secularity is the awareness of our full responsibility upon coming of age. The mystery here is the intersection between immanence and transcendence.

Even at the risk of possible misunderstanding (should my words be interpreted only in one key), I would try to express what can be considered a true humanization within the framework of these three major human traditions. Humanizing Man means to make "Man" truly human, but the expression is treacherous and ambivalent because this gerund is neither merely transitive nor merely intransitive. It is not as if someone else were humanizing us or as if we ourselves could achieve what we are not yet. Humanizing "Man" means rather this plunge into reality and participation in the overall destiny of all that is, which takes place inside and outside each of us. It is a process by which each becomes truly a person, sometimes abandoning the image we have of ourselves, dying, disappearing, transcending ourselves; other times affirming our being when it is threatened by alien forces, but in every case entering into a deeper *ontonomic* relationship with Reality—whatever this may be or not be. It is touching not only the shore of gentleness, power, and wisdom but also the depths of despair, nothingness, and death. It is to be all that we are uniquely capable of; it cannot be compared to anything else. Each person is a unique knot in the universal net. It means to reach the heights of the

Godhead if this is the model we have of ourselves, provided such a vocation is not merely a wishful projection of lower unfulfilled desires. It means for us to touch the shore of nothingness, provided we do not rest in that nonexisting place. It means to develop all the human potentialities, provided these are not artificially concocted dreams. It means finally to know and accept the human predicament and, at the same time, to recognize that this very human predicament carries with it the constant overcoming of all that human beings are now.[127]

It is in this sense that today the sincere and totally (because disinterestedly) committed *studium* of religion, with all its attendant risks, uncertainties, and joys, is perhaps one of the most authentic religious acts—at least for some of us.

NOTES

1. The nature of this chapter, I hope, justifies omitting so-called secondary literature—otherwise so helpful—and limiting quotations to just indicative samples. Most of the citations are taken from the author's books: *The Silence of God* (Maryknoll, N.Y.: Orbis, 1989; completely revised and enlarged ed.; *El silencio del Buddha* [Madrid: Siruela, 1996]); and *Humanismo y Cruz* (Madrid: Rialp, 1963).

2. Cf. R. Panikkar, "Have 'Religions' the Monopoly on *Religion?*" *Journal of Ecumenical Studies*, 11:3 (Summer, 1974), pp. 515–17.

3. I.e., the doctrine of the nonself or of the ultimate unsubstantiality of the being. Cf., for example, *Samyutta-nikāya* III, 66; *Dīgha-nikāya* II, 64 sq.; *Milindapañha* II, 1, 1 (or 251); II, 2, 1; III 5, 6; et al.

4. The four noble truths or *aryasaccāni* (in Sanskrit, *āryasatyāni*), namely: the universal fact of sorrow, the different cravings as the cause of sorrow, the stopping of all cravings as the stopping of sorrow, and the eightfold path leading out of sorrow: right vision, right intention, right discourse, right behavior, right livelihood, right effort, right memory, and right concentration. Cf. *Samyutta-nikāya* V, 420 sq.

5. I.e., all conditioned things (*samkhāra*) are sorrow. Cf. *Dhammapada* XX, 6 (Nr. 278). Suffering, un-easiness, turmoil are other versions of *duḥkham* (from the root *duṣ*, deteriorate).

6. Cf. *Mahāparinibbāna-sutta* VI, 10; III, 66; et al. Cf., incidentally, Phil. 2:12: "You must work out your own salvation in fear and trembling."

7. Gen. I:1 sq.; I:31; et al.

8. Cf. Lk. II:11; Acts XIII:23; et al.

9. Cf. Jn. I:14; et al.

10. Cf. Deut. VI:5.

11. Cf. Mt. XXII:37-40.

12. The Pāli *taṇhā* corresponds to the Sanskrit *tṛṣṇā,* meaning thirst. Besides the text already quoted, cf. *Aṅguttara-nikāya* III, 416; IV, 400; *Saṁyutta-nikāya* I, 1; I, 8; *Majjhima-nikāya* I, 6; II, 256; *Itivuttaka* 30; 50; 58; 105; et al.

13. The New Testament term is *epithymia,* which Latin theology translated by *concupiscentia.* Cf. 1 Jn. II:16–17; 2 Pet. II:18; Gal. V:16; Rom. VI:12; 2 Tim. III:6; et al.

14. Cf. *Majjhima-nikāya* III, 6, et al.: "The Tathāgata limits himself to show the path;" et al. (cf. also *Majjhima-nikāya* I, 83).

15. Cf. Jn. X:9; XIV:6; et al.

16. Cf. *Milindapañha* 326; et al.

17. Cf. Jn. XVI:8 sq.; XVII:9 sq.; et al.

18. Cf. *Udāna* V, 5: "As, O bhikkhus, the great ocean has but one single taste, the salty taste, even so, O bhikkhus, the discipline of the teaching has but one single taste, the taste of liberation. That the discipline of the teaching, O bhikkhus, has a single taste, the taste of liberation, this is, O bhikkhus, the sixth marvelous and extraordinary thing of the discipline of the teaching." Cf. the same metaphor in CU VI, 13 for a different, but related, teaching. Cf. also Jn. VIII:36; 1 Pet. II:16; Rom. VIII:21; et al., for the christian side.

19. The word is not exclusively buddhist, as is proved by the BG II, 72; VI, 15; the MB XIV, 543; et al.; and confirmed by the discussions on the nonbuddhist meanings of the term in *Digha-nikāya* I, 3; 19; etc.

20. The word is on the one hand the greek rendering of the hebrew *yeshuah, yesha,* and *yoshuah,* and on the other the christian rendering of the same word of classical antiquity; often ambivalent, i.e., applied to Gods and Men alike.

21. Cf. *Saṁyutta-nikāya* II, 68.

22. I.e., "of all this-worldly elements," "of all creatureliness" one could venture to translate. Cf. ibid. I, 136.

23. Cf. ibid. I, 210.

24. Cf. ibid. I, 39.

25. Cf. the etymology of *nirvāṇa:* from the intransitive verb *nirvā,* be extinct, consumed. The root *vā* means blow, *vāta* means wind (cf. *spiritus, pneuma*). *Nirvāṇa* is the extinction of all combustible (mortal, contingent, temporal) material.

26. Cf. *Kathavatthu* XIX, 6.

27. Cf. *Itivuttaka* II, 6 (or 43); *Udāna* VIII, 3.

28. Cf. *Udāna* VIII, 1.

29. Cf. Nāgārjuna, *Mūlamādhyamakakārikā* XXV, 1 sq.

30. Cf. Candrakīrti, *Prasannapadā* XXIV, *passim.*

31. Cf. the entire chapter III or *suññatavagga of Majjhima-nikāya.*

32. Cf. the famous parable of the man wounded by the arrow who dies, having wasted his time inquiring after such unnecessary details as who shot it and why, in *Majjhima-nikāya* 1,426 sq.; *Aṅguttara-nikāya* IV, 67 sq.

33. Cf. *Majjhima-nikāya* III, 254, where concentration is called void, signless, and aimless.

34. *Udāna* VIII, 3. Cf. also Candrakīrti, *Prasannapadā* XXV, 3 (ed. La Vallée Poussin; tr. R.H. Robinson, p. 521): "Nirvāṇa is defined as un-abandoned, unattained, unannihilated, non-eternal, unextinguished, unarisen."

35. This could be considered the quintessence of Nāgārjuna's insight.

36. Cf. the important concept of *asaṁskṛta*, the nonconstructed. The notion of *akata (akṛta)* , the not-done, -made, -created, stands in contraposition to the *saṁskṛta*, the constructed, of the indic tradition. Cf. *Dhammapada* VII, 8 (97).

37. Cf. Phil. I:28.

38. Cf. 2 Cor. VII:10.

39. Cf. 1 Th. V:9; et al.

40. Cf. Heb. II:10.

41. Cf. Heb. V:9.

42. Cf. 1 Pet. I:9–10.

43. Cf. Jn. IV:22.

44. Cf. Acts XVI:17.

45. Cf. Acts XIII:26; et al.

46. Cf. Lk. I:77.

47. Cf. Lk. II:11 and the very name Jesus *(Yoshua)* which means salvation.

48. Cf. Mt. I:21; Acts V:31.

49. Cf. Acts IV:12.

50. The root *śū (śvid)* means 'swell'. Betty Heimann repeatedly points out that *śūnya* and *śūna*, the void and the swollen (the excessive), both come from the same root *śun*. Nirvāṇa is also called *kṛtsham*, the whole, or *śukla*, the indiscriminate whiteness. *Facets of Indian Thoughts* (London: Allen & Unwin, 1964), pp. 100, 110–11. The term *śūnya* (empty or void) exists already in ancient prebuddhist and nonbuddhist literature. Cf. AV XIV, 2, 19; SB II, 3, 1, 9; TB II, 1, 2, 12; and many Upaniṣad. An interesting compound is *śūnyāgāra*, the deserted, empty house (JabU VI), signifying the house where the *saṁnyāsīs* or hindu monks were supposed to live (or also in a dwelling place of the God, a temple: *devagṛha*). Cf. also MaitU VI, 10.

51. There is no need to stress that *plêrôma*—i.e., that which fills (up)—is of prechristian origin and has its full meaning in greek literature.

52. Cf. the beginning of Nāgārjuna's *Mūlamadhyamikakārikā* I, 1: "Neither out of themselves, nor out of something else, nor out of any cause, do existing things arise."

53. Cf. the expression *svabhāvaśūnyatā* (emptiness of [in] its own being) as one mode of emptiness described in the *Pañcaviṁśatisāhasrikā* (one of the later Prajñāpāramitā-sūtra), or the expression *svabhāvaśūnya* as the quintessence of the *Prajñāpāramitā*. Cf. also the *dharmaśūnyatā* of Śāntideva's *Sikṣāsamuccaya* XIV, 242 and the *śūnyabhutaḥ* (void of being) of the MaitU VI, 23.

54. The simile of the other shore is recurrent in buddhist literature. Cf. *Aṅguttara-nikāya* II, 24; IV, 13; IV, 160; *Itivuttaka* 69; *Saṁyutta-nikāya* IV, 175; *Prajñāpāramitā-sūtra* IX; et al.

55. Cf. Nāgārjuna, *Mūlamadhyamakakārikā* XXV, 19.

56. Were there any difference between the two, this would be *saṃsāra* or *nirvāṇa* of some third thing, each of which is contradictory.

57. Cf. *Lalitavistara* XIII, 175 sq. *Majjhima-nikāya* I, 297, stresses that the world is empty (in pāli, *suñña*) of self and of what pertains to the self *(attā* and *attaniya).* Cf. also *Saṃyutta-nikāya* IV, 54 and 296; et al.

58. Cf. *Saṃyutta-nikāya* III, 189.

59. Cf. Eph. IV:13; et al.

60. God sent his Son at the fullness of time *(chronos)* (Gal. IV:4), but in the fullness of times *(kairos)* he will gather all things in Christ (Eph. I:10).

61. Cf. Eph. I:23.

62. Cf. Jn. I:16.

63. Col. II:9.

64. Cf. Eph. III:19.

65. Cf. Acts III:21.

66. Cf. 1 Cor. XV:28.

67. Cf. Mt. V:48.

68. Cf. Jn. XV:1 sq.

69. Cf. Jn. VI:56–57; XVII:23; et al.

70. Cf. Gen. III:5.

71. Cf. Jn. I:12 (and, with qualifications, X:34–35); et al.

72. Cf. Jn. XIV:17; XV:26; et al.

73. Cf. Clement of Alexandria, *Proptrepticus* I, 9 (here using *theopoieīn* which generally referred to the making of idols); Gregory of Nazianzus, *Oratio theologica* III, 19 (P. G., 36, 100); Athanasius: Αὐτὸς γὰρ ἐνηνθρώπησεν, ἵνα ἡμεῖς θεοποιηθῶμεν; "Ipse siquidem homo factus est, ut nos dii efficeremur," (For he was made Man that we might be made God) *De Incarnatione Verbi* 54 (P. G., 25, 192); *Oratio 4 contra arrianos* VI (P. G., 26, 476); Augustine, *Sermo* 128 (P. L., 39, 1997); *Sermo de Nativitate* 3 and 11 (P. L., 38, 99 and 1016); "Propter te factus est temporalis, ut tu fias aeternus," says Augustine in his lapidary style, *Epist. Io.* II, 10 (P. L., 35, 1994); "Quod est Christus, erimus christiani," repeats Cyprian, *De idolorum vanitate* XV (P. L., 4, 582); et al.

74. Cf. Rev. XXI:1.

75. Cf. 1 Cor. XV:12 sq.

76. Cf. Jn. III:3 sq.

77. Cf. Mt. IV:17; et al.

78. Cf. Mt. III:2; et al.

79. Cf. Śāntideva, *Bodhicaryāvatāra* IX, 49.

80. Cf. Candrakīrti, *Prasannapadā* XVI, 8 (ed. La Vallée Poussin, p. 293).

81. *Prajñā, śūnyatā, pratītyasamutpāda, nirvāṇa.*

82. *Udāna* I, 10.

83. Cf. the famous saying of Pascal, *Pensées,* 358: "L'homme n'est ni ange ni bête, et le malheur veut que qui veut faire l'ange fait la bête."

84. Cf. the oft-quoted passage, "Agnosce, O christiane, dignitatem tuam, et divinae consors factus naturae, noli in veterem vilitatem degeneri conversarione redire. Memento cuius capitis et cuius corporis sis membrum," Leo I, *Sermo* 21, 3 (P. L., 54, 192–93).

85. Cf. the famous augustinian "irrequietum est cor nostrum donec requiescat in te." *Confess.* I, 1, 1.

86. Cf. Maximus Confessor, *Ambigua,* "God has inserted in the human heart the desire of him" (P. G., 91, 1312); or, accepting the idea that a purified *epithymia* (consupiscence) can become the burning desire of him, *Quaest. ad Thal.* (P. G., 90, *269).* Cf. the christian commentary on Jn. VI:44: "Nemo te quaerere valet nisi qui prius invenerit," Bernard of Clairvaux, *De diligendo Deo* VII, 22 (P. L, 182, 987); also, "Console-toi, tu ne me chercherais pas, si tu ne m'avais pas trouvé." Pascal, *Pensées,* 553.

87. Cf. 2 Pet. I:4; et al.

88. Cf. Rom. VIII:29; et al.

89. Cf. Heb. II:11; et al.

90. Cf. Gal. IV:5; et al.

91. Cf. I Jn. II:29; et al.

92. Cf. Jn. III:5; et al.

93. Πάντων χημάτων μέτρον ἄνθρωπος, Protagoras, *Frag.* 1.

94. Cf. Plato, *Cratylus,* 386a; *Theatetus,* 152a.

95. Cf. Plato, *Laws* IV (716 c).

96. Cf. Aristotle, *Nicomachean Ethics* X, 7 (1177 b 31).

97. Literally: ἦθος ἀνθρώπῳ δαίμων—"The ethos to Man (is his) *daimōn."* Heraclitus, *Frag.* 119.

98. Cf. Gen. I:26–27.

99. This could be said to be the theological justification of all humanisms of a biblical origin.

100. Cf. Jn. I:14.

101. Cf. Jn. XIX:5.

102. Cf. the famous *avyakṛtavastuni,* or unutterable things, which the Buddha refused to answer. Cf. the *vacchagotta saṁyuttam (Saṁyutta-nikāya* III, 33), *avyakata saṁyuttam (Saṁyutta-nikāya* IV, *44), cūlamāluṅkya sutta (Majjhima-nikāya* 63), the *aggivacchagotta sutta (Majjhima-nikāya* 72), etc.

103. Cf., for instance, Buddha's refusal to elaborate on the nature of *karma* because the only thing that matters is getting rid of it. Cf. *Aṅguttara-nikāya* II, 80; *Digha-nikāya* III, 138; *Saṁyutta-nikāya* III, 103.

104. That the Buddha "has no theories" *(Majjhima-nikāya* I, 486) is a constant idea in the buddhist canon, later converted in the Madhyāmika into the central message of buddhism.

105. RV X, 90, 2.

106. Cf. SU III, 8 sq.; et al.

107. This reference to the chinese world is meant to signify that no complete

and valid discourse on humanization can take place today without including what is perhaps the most humane of all cultures, whose ideal has always been the perfect Man. Cf. a single example, which may well be considered representative of more than one tradition: "Therefore the Perfect Man makes his spirit and mind penetrate the limitless and cannot be impeded by limits, pushes to the utmost the sight and hearing of eye and ear and cannot be contrained by sound and forms—because he identifies with the self voidness of the myriad things. Thus, things cannot hinder his spirit-intelligence." Seng-Chao, *Emptiness of the Non-Absolute* (Chao-lun III; tr. R.H. Robinson).

108. No point in giving here a bibliography that would cover more pages than our entire chapter.

109. Cf. the well-known *splendida vitia* of Augustine for the "virtues" of those not reborn in baptism; and again, "Bene currunt; sed in via non currunt. Quanto plus currunt, plus errant; quia a via recedunt," *Sermo* 141, c. 4, nr. 4 (P. L., 38, 777); or again, "maius opus est ut ex impio justus fiat, quam creare caelum et terram," *In Ioh.* tr. 72, nr. 3 (P. L, 35, 1823), commented upon by Thomas, "Bonum gratiae unius maius est quam bonum naturae totius universi" *(Sum. theol.* I-II, q. 113, a. 9, c. et ad 2); and again, developed in his own way by Meister Eckhart in his *Serm. lat.* II, 2 *(Lateinische Werke* IV, 16,n. 10); et al.

110. Cf. the etymological hint: *Saeculum* is certainly not the *kosmos,* but rather the *aiôn,* the life span (cf. the Sanskrit *āyus*), i.e., the temporal aspect of the world.

111. We say one-sided because it cannot be denied that the traditional answers have not taken into account the whole of the human horizon; in our kairological moment, this is imperative.

112. Needless to say, we can only indicate in a general way how fundamental research on this problem could be started.

113. In point of fact, *karuṇā* and *śūnyatā* are the two pillars of mahāyāna, and many texts link them.

114. Cf. the well-known "tu autem eras interior intimo meo et superior summo meo" of Augustine *(Confessions* III, 6, 11). Cf. also Thomas, *Sum. theol.,* I, q. 8, a. 1; I,q. 105, a. 5; Calvin, *Institutiones christianae religionis* III, 7: "Quod si nostri non sumus, sed Domini . . . ergo ne vel ratio nostra, vel voluntas in consiliis nostris factisque dominetur (. . .) Nostri non sumus: ergo quoad licet obliviscamur nosmetipsos ac nostra omnia. Rursum, Dei sumus: illi ergo vivamus et moriamur," *(Opera Calvini,* ed. Brunsvigae, 1864, vol. 2, col. 505–6); not to mention the mystics.

115. Cf. Acts XVII:28.

116. Cf. Jn. XVII:22–26; et al.

117. Cf. 2 Cor. V:17; Gal. VI:15; Eph. IV:24; Col. III:10; et al.

118. Interestingly enough, the buddhist intuition of *nairātmyavāda* tallies in an astounding way with the christian doctrine of the *perichôrêsis (circumincessio).*

119. Cf. Thomas, *Sum. theol.,* I, q. 1, a. 8 ad 2; I, q. 2, a'. 2 ad 1; although Aquinas does not use the literal words of this later famous principle.

120. Any humanism entails an affirmation of Man that transcends the "Man" who affirms it.

121. Cf. R. Panikkar, "Some Notes on Syncretism and Eclecticism related to the Growth of Human Consciousness" in *Religious Syncretism in Antiquity. Essays in Conversation with Geo. Widengren,* edited by Birger A. Pearson (Missoula, Montana: Scholars Press, 1975), pp. 47–60.

122. A recurrent theme of the Buddha's teachings is that they do not have authority of their own, but only inasmuch as the hearer experiences them as conveying a real message of liberation. Cf. the buddhist tradition: "Those who fantasize about the Buddha, who is beyond fancies and imperishable, are all slain by fancy and do not see the *Tathāgata*" (Candrakīrti, *Prasannapadā* XXII, 15 [ed. La Vallée Poussin, tr. R.H. Robinson, p. 448]).

123. This goes to the extreme of: "Kill the Buddha if you happen to meet him!" *Taishō Tripitaka* 47,500b (*apud* K. Ch'en, *Buddhism in China.* Princeton: Princeton University Press, 1964, p. 358).

124. Cf. Mk. II:27.

125. Cf. Rom. VIII:21; et al.

126. Cf. Jn. VIII:32.

127. Cf. the *Sermo I* of C.G. Jung's *VII Sermones ad mortuos* printed privately in 1916 and published as Appendix to his Autobiography: *Erinnerungen, Träume, Gedanken* edited by A. Jaffé, (Olten-Freiburg: Walter, 1972), pp. 389 sq. Some excerpts: "Das Nichts oder die Fülle nennen wir das *Pleroma* [where the greek-christian terminological bias is apparent]. Dort drin hört denken und sein auf, denn das ewige und unendliche hat keine eigenschaften." [*sic* with the capitals]

10

Toward a Hindu-Christian Dialogue

THE HINDU-CHRISTIAN DIALOGUE IS NOT A MERELY THEO-
retical issue. It belongs to the life of the peoples of the world, and of
the indic subcontinent in particular. Many historical movements today are
not only incomprehensible but would have been impossible without this
mutual fecundation between religions, hinduism and christianity in this
case. History is not only an account of wars. Che Guevara and Martin
Luther King, Jr., are impossible without Gandhi, who is indebted to Tol-
stoy, who in turn is the product of an eastern christianity that has one of
its roots in eastern spiritualities of an extra- and prechristian nature. The
great names of the school of Alexandria were strongly influenced by indic
doctrines. Pantaenus went to India; Ammonius Saccas, whatever his origin, was conversant with oriental religions. . . . There is a *mālā*, a rosary of
living names, East and West, hindu and christian, that forms the warp and
woof of real human history. In short, the Desert Fathers and the hindu

mystics as much as the british viceroys and the hindu rajas or muslim nawabs are latent partners in the present-day encounters.

Mahatma Gandhi, when addressing a group of christians in 1927, told them to use hindi instead of english and to give the spinning wheel priority over literacy in uplifting the masses; Gandhi thus touched on two of the most fundamental pillars for dialogue: *language* and *praxis.*

Dialogue, to begin with, has to be *duo-logue.* There have to be two logoi, two languages encountering each other, so as to overcome the danger of a double monologue. One has to know the language of the other, even if one has to learn it precisely from the other, and often in the very exercise of dialogue. Dialogue engages the intellect, the Logos. The academic study of religion is not a luxury.

At the same time, it has to be *dia-logue,* that is, a piercing of the Logos, an overcoming of the mere intellectual level, a going *through* the intellect into an encounter of the whole person. It has to proceed from praxis and discover the symbolic power of action.

The dialogue comes from the heart of the people and is situated in the middle of life. The spinning wheel is the symbol of Gandhi's challenge to technocracy and the way of saying that the hindu-christian dialogue has to proceed starting from both sides. Many present-day dialogues set the stage according to the terms of one of the parties alone. To assume that christocentrism—or theocentrism, for that matter—can offer a basis is as unsatisfactory as to presume that *apauruṣeyatva* (that which is not man-made, such as 'scriptures')—or *karman* for that matter—are proper starting points. But there is a much more subtle partner for fruitful and unbiased dialogue: modernity.

The modern kosmology (*sic*), which assumes that time is linear, that history is paramount, that individuality is the essence of Man, that democracy is an absolute, that technocracy is neutral, that social darwinism is valid, and so on, cannot offer a fair platform for the dialogue. The basis for the dialogue cannot be the modern western myth. As I have explained elsewhere, we face here a "conflict of kosmologies." Religions are not only doctrines, and even doctrines have roots in the respective myths that make the doctrines plausible. Modern Science has permeated the modern world to such an extent that it is difficult to avoid taking it as the basis of the dialogue. Both hinduism and christianity have to come to grips with modern science, but it would not be fair to hinduism to consider modern science as the neutral starting point. Though modern science is not christianity, both share many common myths extraneous to the hindu traditions. One can understand a certain hindu resistance to an apparently neutral dialogue based on the assumptions of a scientific kosmology.

In other words, a complete *dialogos* should be at the same time a *diamythos.* The respective logoi are bearers of meaning and life only within their respective *mythoi,* and it is by means of dialogue that we reach the myth of the other and create a climate of communication. To mention the mythos belongs certainly to a prologue introducing the *dialogue.* The mythos is that which goes before the Logos and makes it possible. The *pro-logue,* the foreword, belongs to the mythos. The Unsaid, which is taken for granted. . . .

How often have academics forgotten, if not despised, the spinning wheel! How often have communal riots and cold wars persisted through the ages because people have forgotten, if not despised, learning the language of the other! Language here means, of course, more than hindi, and the spinning wheel more than *khadi.*

I would like to stress here a not-so-insignificant result of the hindu-christian dialogue. In spite of misunderstandings, difficulties, and drawbacks, it has an unavoidable effect: It changes not only our opinion of the religion we study and dialogue with; it also changes our stand and interpretation of our own religion. It undermines, as it were, the very basis on which one stood when beginning the dialogue. The dialogue, even if imperfectly undertaken, backfires. We may not convince the partners; we may even get irritated at the others; they may be impervious to our opinions. Nevertheless, we ourselves imperceptibly change our stance. The interreligious dialogue triggers the intrareligious dialogue in our own minds and hearts. Indeed, the dialogue backfires. . . . I would like to expand briefly on what this implies.

What follows offers only a nonfuturistic thought, first from a psychological and then a sociological perspective.

A good number of factors have changed in the present-day historical constellation:

1. Both hinduism and christianity have lost political power. India is no longer dominated by a christian empire, nor is she legally controlled by hindu institutions. Both hindus and christians still have to overcome mutual suspicions and heal wounds of the past, but the meeting can take place without direct political interference.

2. Both hinduism and christianity are undergoing an institutional crisis, and this creates fellowship when the hindus sense that the same difficulties and struggles are also felt by the christians, and vice-versa.

3. Both religions are also facing a similar challenge from the technocratic complex. The challenge is not the same, nor is it seen in the same way, but nevertheless it is there. Traditional religions are not the most exciting aspects of modern life, for the burgeoning middle class at least. This puts people interested in traditional religions in the same boat, as it were. I am not saying that we strengthen our links by recounting our mutual woes and fears or that we should be crusading against a common opponent. I am saying that the platform for the dialogue is changing.

4. Something similar could be said regarding marxism or humanism.

5. Due to many reasons, at least some of them having to do with the above-mentioned points, both religions are on the brink of a mutation, different as the two mutations may be. Perhaps the key word here is *secularity*. At any rate, there is a reinterpretation of tradition and a reformulation of the main tenets of both religions or, as I have said, of those bundles of religions that we gather under these two generic names. This puts the dialogue in a very peculiar and fruitful position. Unless we are going to discuss, say, what Śaṅkara and Aquinas wrote, that is, unless we are engaging in merely historical and exegetical research, when we come together ready for a dialogue we do not know much. Not only do we not know what the other is going to say, but we don't even know what we ourselves are going to be elicited to articulate. The dialogue does not take place from two firm and well-delimited trenches; rather, it is an open field. How often one has heard the criticism from the other side: "But you as a hindu (or a christian) should not be saying this." Yet we are saying it. I am not saying that dogmas do not exist. I am affirming that dogmatism is not needed and that even dogmas are on the move. Saying this, I am at the same time uncovering for the dialogue a task beyond the already important tasks of understanding each other or dispelling misunderstanding. I am ascribing to the dialogue the important role of building a new self-understanding of both traditions.

I foresee a new and fundamental function of dialogue in the encounter of religions. The first aim was to better know each other, to dispel fears and misinterpretations. A second role was that of mutual influence and fecundation. I envisage now a third function: that of positively contributing to the new self-understanding of both sides. If this is the case, the dialogue will become an indispensable element in the very formation of the new identity of each religious tradition. We shall no longer sit facing each other, but sitting at a truly round table, or sitting cross-legged side-by-side (following the two physical ways of sitting), we will discuss together the deepening of our insights. The revolution this would accomplish should be apparent to all.

Let me underline in a more systematic way what I have called the four phases of the hindu-christian dialogue.

The first phase could be described as the period in which hindus were the dominating power. All too often the history of Kerala christians has been judged from the perspective of the second phase, that in which christians had the power, although they were not in the majority. All too often, also, the hindu reactions to an overwhelming christian domination have not been sufficiently underlined.

I am saying that the hindu-christian dialogue has never been a round-table conference, not a merely theoretical exercise in *brahmodya* (theological disputations). It is embedded in particular sociopolitical circumstances and takes place within a certain elusive myth.

The first phase was that of a tiny minority finding its own identity: christians dialoging with the hindu majority in order to establish their own identity. No wonder the dialogue was not one of the great theological speculations, as it has been noted. It was the *christian* dialogue with hinduism.

The second phase reverses the roles. Demographically, the hindus were the majority, of course, but the power was on the other side. Hinduism had to establish its identity and awaken from an alleged slumber that had permitted first the muslim and later the christian conquests. The so-called hindu renaissance is witness thereof. It was a *hindu* dialogue with christianity.

The third phase is the prevalent one today in religious and academic circles. It could only flourish after the colonial period. It is the *hindu-christian* dialogue. Christians, to be sure, have taken most of the initiative, and it has been a predominantly *christian-hindu* dialogue; but hindu voices are also present and many of the christians have adopted an unpartisan stance. It has been a predominantly doctrinal dialogue. Christian doctrines have been deepened, enlarged, or perhaps also stretched thin for the sake of the dialogue. Hindu doctrines have been awakened so as to show that there was also 'science', 'rationality', service of neighbor, and the like in hindu lore. Comparative studies of great value have appeared. Śaṅkara and Aquinas; Kṛṣṇa and Christ; hindu and christian pilgrimages; the notion of grace; scriptures, God, and so forth, are today well-studied topics. But comparative studies are only implicit dialogues.

This third phase has eliminated clichés of superiority, exclusivism, and absolutism from both sides—exceptions notwithstanding. Schopenhauer and Hegel, for example, read all the available hindu materials of their times. Yet their knowledge of hinduism today seems insufficient. Vivekananda and Aurobindo, similarly, had sympathy for christianity and were somewhat informed. Yet their knowledge of christian theology was rudimentary. It is to the credit of this third phase that it has created a more conducive climate for dialogue. Here one has to acknowledge the great services of academic studies.

But I envision a distinctive fourth phase. The fourth phase, I submit, challenges the fixed identity of both parties. The fecundation of the previous phases has produced its effects. The fourth phase is a genuine dialogue among people who happen to be hindus and christians. It is the *religious dialogue* among hindus and christians. Let me elaborate on this.

"As a hindu, I have never found it difficult to identify with the person of Jesus," writes Anantanand Rambachan in typical fashion. To which I personally could add: As a christian (and I insist on the lower case), I have no difficulty in identifying myself with the hindu *dharma*.

Colleagues from both sides will rightly remark that it all depends on what we understand by Jesus and *dharma*. Jesus, whose 'person', according to the first christian councils, is not human but divine? The Risen Christ, as St. Paul believes? What Jesus? *Dharma*, as Manu describes it? Or, as the *svadharma* of the Gītā? The sanātana *dharma* of neohinduism?

But here the problems begin and do not end. What does it mean to be a hindu? Or a christian? Is it a doctrine, an interpretation? A church or *sampradāya*? A historical tradition? Is is party line? What makes one a hindu? Or a christian? Who decides? And even if we say a community, which one? And according to which criteria? Have we to prescribe once and for all what it is to be a hindu or a christian? Are all the meat eaters bad hindus? And all the nonchurchgoers bad christians?

The hindu-christian dialogue is not exhausted with the comparison between Rāmānuja and Bonaventure—important as those and similar studies are.

The dialogue has to be secular; it has to descend to the areas of mutual concern; it has to enter into the human and political arena of our times. But the understanding of the *saeculum* does not need to be the christian notion of secularization. We need to unearth the underlying kosmologies.

The fourth phase starts a dialogue in which neither a politically dominating hinduism nor an established and powerful christianity has the upper hand or provides the framework in which the dialogue takes place. Nor is the dialogue purely dialectical or simply doctrinal. The dialogue has gone deeper, on the one hand, and gotten more external, on the other. Deeper, for we discuss personal issues and beliefs with immense consequences for our lives. More external, for we do not involve large communities or speak from the definite position of a church or *samprādaya*. Both sides seem to be confronted with a similar technocratic civilization, even in the remote corners of the countryside.

It would amount to a superficial stance and possibly to a betrayal of one's deepest convictions, were we to deal with modern problems of technocracy, peace, justice, hunger, or simply business and work in such a way that we make abstraction of religious beliefs or relegate them to the private sphere. The hindu and christian contexts are different; they are religious and personal, but at the same time political, economic, and secular, and they inform ordinary life. Do we need an Ayatollah Khomeini to remind us brutally that one side alone does not set the rules of the game? The fourth phase of the dialogue is a burning issue. The quick rise of an indian middle class apparently successful in the rules of a competitive society in a technocratic system is not an alien problem to the hindu-christian dialogue. It becomes a necessary part of dialogue—perhaps even for survival.

This fourth phase is, first of all, dialogue. It is a dialogue among experts or common people, merchants or industrialists, intellectuals or artists who happen to more or less love their traditions, but who are not tied to them to such an extent that they defend any fixed orthodoxy. The archetypes may play a more important role than the explicit ideas. To be sure, any authentic dialogue is a search for truth, and therefore it runs the 'risk' of finding itself 'outside' the fold. But in this emerging fourth phase there are no nonnegotiable topics, no 'classified' materials or hidden agendas, not because previously people were not sincere, but because the very notion of orthodoxy has become flexible, dynamic, and not merely intellectual.

It would be a setback in the dialogue if this fourth phase were to be lured into the trap of superficiality. The fourth phase is a new step. It is creative not only in interpreting the 'other'. It is also innovative in understanding 'oneself'.

I could put it in terms of depth psychology. Should not a christian, after twenty years of studying hinduism—and a hindu, after a similar period of struggling with christianity—assume that in an imperceptible way the studied subject matter has made inroads into their respective psyches, just as one spontaneously imitates the gestures and idioms of the persons one lives with? Should we not suspect also that one may one day fall in love with the person with whom one is constantly dealing? Cultural symbiosis is also a phenomenon happening among religious traditions. We also know that the constant encounter with each other may generate hatred and disgust, or sometimes sheer indifference. Fundamental reactions are also possible. But we should overcome religious nationalisms *pari pasu* so that we may walk toward a healthy pluralism.

Index of Scriptures

Index of Names

Index of Subjects

Acknowledgments

G RATEFUL ACKNOWLEDGMENT IS MADE TO THE EDITORS AND publishers of the following books and journals for granting permission to use materials that appeared in them. All the chapters, however, have been revised for this book.

Motto Appeared in *Journal of Ecumenical Studies* 21, 4, p. 773.

Chapter 1 Revised version of the first edition.

Chapter 2 Appeared in F. Whaling (ed.), *The World's Religion Traditions* (Edinburgh: T. & T. Clark, 1984), pp. 201–21.

Chapter 3 Revised version of "Fe y creencia. Sobre la experiencia multireligiosa. Un fragmento autobiográfico objetivado." *Homenaje a Xavier Zubiri* (Madrid: Moneda y Crèdito, 1970), vol. 2, pp. 435–59. A shorter version appeared as: "A Multireligious Experience. An Objectified Autobiographical Fragment." *Anglican Theological Review* 53, No. 4 (October 1971).

Chapter 4 Appeared in *The Journal of Religious Studies* (Punjabi University) 3, 1 (1971), pp. 12–16.

Chapter 5 Appeared in *Religion and Society* 15, 3 (1968), pp. 55–66.

Chapter 6 Appeared in *The Harvard Theological Review* 66, 1 (January 1973), pp. 113–14.

Chapter 7 Appeared in *Journal of Ecumenical Studies* 19, 4, pp. 781–86.

Chapter 8 Appeared in *Catalonia* 43 (1955), pp. 32–35.

Chapter 9 Appeared in J. M. Robinson (ed.), *Religion and the Humanizing of Man* (Waterloo, Ont., Canada: Council on the Study of Religion, 1972), pp. 67–86.

Chapter 10 From a Foreword to H. Coward (ed.), *Hindu-Christian Dialogue* (Maryknoll: Orbis, 1990).

Works by Raimon Panikkar on Dialogue

Books

1963/VII.   *L'incontro delle religioni nel mondo contemporaneo* (Rome: Edizioni Internacionali Sociali).

1963/VIII.   *Die vielen Götter und der eine Herr* (Weilheim/Obb.: o.w. Barth).

1964/IX.   *Religione e religioni* (Brescia: Morcelliana).

1966/XII.   *Mâyâ e Apocalisse* (Rome: Abete).

1967/13.   *Kerygma und Indien* (Hamburg: Reich).

1967/XIV.   *Offenbarung und Verkündigung* (Freiburg: Herder).

1970/XI.   *Le mystère du culte dans l'hindouisme et le christianisme* (Paris: Cerf).

1981/X.   *The Unknown Christ of Hinduism* (Maryknoll: Orbis).

1990/XXX.   *Sobre el diálogo intercultural* (Salamanca: San Esteban).

1995/XLI.   *Invisible Harmony* (Minneapolis: Fortress).

Articles

1967/10.   "Dialogue between Ian and Ray: Is Jesus Christ Unique?" *Theoria to Theory*, Cambridge, I, pp. 127–37.

1972/3.   "Il dialogo come atto religioso" *Rocca*, Assisi, 31, 2, pp. 15–17.

1979/1.   "Ṛtatattva: A Preface to a Hindu-Christian Theology" *Jeevadara*, Kottayam, 9, 29, pp. 6–63.

1983/8.   "Per un dialogo delle civiltà," Dibattituto tenutosi a Città di Castello il 22-9-1982. Città di Castello (Centro Studi l'Altrapagina), 28 pp. (pro manuscripto).

1985/19.   "Hinduism and Christ," in *In Spirit and in Truth* (essays dedicated to Fr. Ignatius Hirudayan), ed. Viyagappa, Madras (Aikiya Alayam), pp. 112–22.

1990/7.   "La sfida dell'incontro planetario tra i popoli," in *Rivolgimenti. Dialoghi di fine millennio*, ed. Marco Guzzi (Genova: Marietti), pp. 16–36.

1991/23. "Begegnung der Religionen: Das unvermeidliche Gespräch" *Dialog der Religionen*, München, I, 1, pp. 9–39.

1994/28. "La mística del diálogo" (Entrevista con R. Panikkar), *Jahrbuch für kontextuelle Theologien 93*, Missionswissenschaftliches Institut, Frankfurt (IKO), 1993, pp. 19–37.

1996/29. "Religión, Filosofía y Cultura," *'Ilu. Rivista de ciencias de las religiones* (Madrid: Universidad Complutense, Instituto Ciencias de las religiones) I, pp. 125–48.

1998/ "El problema de la justicia en el diálogo hindú-cristiano," in *Religiones de la tierra y sacralidad del pobre. Aportación al diálogo interreligioso*, Santander (Sal terrae), pp. 107–35.